About this dictionary

There are many ways to define the field of nar
community work). One way to define it, my favo
It was the politics of narrative practice that drew me to these ideas and ways of working: the politics of gender partnerships to seek to address gender injustice; the politics of developing non-pathologising forms of therapy; the politics of responding to the injustices of Aboriginal deaths in custody and further to question the existence/reliance on prisons; the politics of questioning ourselves, considering how to not only acknowledge privileges but use them well through partnerships and accountabilities; the politics of sponsoring diversity not conformity, and so on.

If you are also drawn to the politics of narrative practice, I hope the diverse entries and stories that you will find within these pages are of interest to you. This political dictionary has been inspired by *A feminist dictionary* compiled by Cheris Kramarae and Paula Treichler back in 1985. *A feminist dictionary* is unlike any other I have turned to. To read it brought challenge, new knowledge, and at times, laughter.

Kramarae and Treichler explicitly acknowledge 'the socio-political aspects of dictionary-making' and at times within one entry offer contradictions without resolving them (pp. 161–162). What's more, they describe how their dictionary was created 'not to authorize but to challenge and envision … (and to) … elucidate and complicate the terms of feminist discourse' (pp. 12–14).

Following their example, this dictionary doesn't seek to authorize a particular version of narrative practice but instead hopes to elucidate and complicate the terms of narrative practice. If you are looking for clear and concise definitions, all written in the same style and voice, I'm sorry but you will not find them here. What you will find are definitions, descriptions, examples, and quotes from multiple authors and perspectives.

This is a partial dictionary in two senses of the term. It is incomplete *and* biased. I have deliberately included entries that emphasise what I consider to be political considerations and dilemmas; tried to amplify some of the more overtly political voices, histories and concepts in the field; and at the same time I've drawn from the Michael White archive some of the political aspects of Michael's work that might otherwise slip from view.

I hope this in some way takes up an invitation that Ron Findlay made in *A memory book for the field of narrative practice*:

> When we are engaging with narrative practices now, I think we shouldn't forget that our therapy practices are also political practices. Like heads and tails, two sides of a coin. For instance, the narrative practice of using people's own words instead of professional definitions can have a positive therapeutic effect, but it is also a political act … of enabling people to represent themselves. If we forget the political history and political side of our practices, we risk losing some of the understanding of them, and we risk making invisible the real political effects of our practices. (Ron Findlay in White, 2016, p. 24)

Of course, as soon as some entries in this (or any other) dictionary are written, they already need updating! I am drawn to the words of genderqueer radical copyeditor Alex Kapitan (2017). In relation to the ways in which the language of gender identity and expression is 'evolving at lightning speed', Alex suggests we:

> Choose to celebrate this rapid evolution of language because of what it means: that people who have been marginalized for centuries are finding ways of reclaiming agency and legitimacy; that those of us who have been written out of existence are finding ways to rewrite reality … The purpose of language is to communicate, not to regulate. (Kapitan, 2017)

The purpose of this incomplete, biased dictionary is also to communicate, not to regulate. If there are entries in these pages that you find helpful, I'd be really interested to hear from you. And if there are omissions, errors, and/or complexities that you notice, I'd love to receive your feedback as well as any additional entries that you and/or your communities might suggest.

How is narrative practice political?

If narrative practice is to be understood as 'political', then how is this politics characterised? And what does this form of politics make possible? The process of compiling this political dictionary has invited, cajoled and finally demanded of me that I clarify my own views about this. In doing so, I have found helpful the following quote from Michel Foucault:

> *I was telling you earlier about the three elements in my morals. They are (1) the refusal to accept as self-evident the things that are proposed to us; (2) the need to analyse and to know, since we can accomplish nothing without reflection and understanding—thus, the principle of curiosity; and (3) the principle of innovation: to seek out in our reflection those things that have never been thought or imagined. Thus: refusal, curiosity, innovation.* (Foucault, 1988a)

Perhaps the politics of narrative practice can be considered through these three principles.

Refusal

Narrative practice, to me, represents a number of refusals. Firstly, a refusal to pathologise or cast people, families or communities as problems. Linked to this, a refusal to participate in the psychologisation of life or traffic in languages of psychoanalysis, psychodynamics, or psychopathology. And furthermore, narrative practice represents a refusal to demonstrate expertise over the lives of others – a refusal to know what is 'healing', 'healthy' or what constitutes a 'good life' for others.

Curiosity

In turning away from interpreting, evaluating or correcting the lives of others, narrative practitioners turn instead toward particular curiosities. This includes a curiosity that supports people to name their experiences in their own words and terms. It also includes a curiosity that seeks to make visible the operations, effects and social histories of problems, including the influence of individual *and* collective histories. This is a curiosity that is open to the ways in which people's stories represent not only personal experience, but also the effects of broader social issues.

A further curiosity associated with narrative practice resurrects and richly describes local knowledges and skills of living that can be brought to bear on local problems. No matter the degree of hardship, individuals, groups and communities will be *responding* to the situations they are in. There will be initiatives they are taking, and skills and knowledges they are using, to try to reduce or redress the harm and/or to care for and protect others.

By exploring how the skills and knowledges of people enduring hardships can make contributions to the lives of others, the person is no longer the problem, the problem is the problem, and the solution becomes not only personal.

From my perspective, the curiosities of narrative practice seek to generate what Michel Foucault described as, 'an insurrection of local knowledges' (1980, p. 81). These forms of curiosity sponsor diversity not conformity and revel in the sacraments of everyday non-conformities.

Innovation

Crucially, rather than being satisfied with critiquing existing pathologising practice, narrative practitioners innovate alternative practices – practices which look different depending on their locations. I am particularly interested in the politics implicit in two sorts of narrative practice innovations.

Partnerships: Inspired by the work of the Just Therapy Team (Waldegrave, Tamasese, Tuhaka & Campbell, 2003), narrative practitioners prioritise the development of innovative partnerships and accountabilities. These partnerships involve recognising and naming privileges and the politics of gender, race, class, age, ethnicity, heterosexism, etc. and create possibilities for collaboratively using privileges and knowledges generated in resistance to marginalisation for social good.

Developing practices most relevant to the most marginalised: Narrative practice began in collaboration with two groups of people whose knowledges are profoundly marginalised within dominant Western culture – young children with emotional/psychological difficulties and adults who had received serious psychiatric diagnoses (see White, 2016). From its origins to today there remains a commitment to innovate forms of practice that are most relevant to the most marginalised.

Of course, dear reader, you may have ideas about further refusals, curiosities and innovations that ought to be included in this list. Or you may propose an entirely different framework!

It's my hope that this political dictionary for the field of narrative practice can spark conversations and debate about the politics of narrative practice. I very much welcome your feedback.

Sources, acknowledgements and inspiration

I have drawn upon diverse sources for the entries within this dictionary. Some of the most helpful have included:

- Cheris Kramarae and Paula Treichler's (1985) *A feminist dictionary*
- *The Michael White Archive*, Dulwich Centre: Kelsi (Sassy) Semeschuk's work as an archivist/researcher was influential in finding quotes from Michael's teaching tapes.
- Alex Kapitan's (2017) *The radical copyeditor's style guide for writing about transgender people*
- Meg-John Barker's (2018) *Good Practice across the Counselling Professions 001 Gender, Sexual, and Relationship Diversity*

Claire Nettle contributed the following entries: insider knowledge; homophobia; narrative justice; normalisation; patriarchal power; post colonialism; and productive power.

Tiffany Sostar offered rigorous critical and creative feedback on an earlier version of this dictionary that has led to its significant improvement. They also contributed to the following entries: accomplice; assigned sex; biphobia; disability, monosexism; intersectionality; open non-monogamies; polyamory and transphobia.

Mary Heath also offered influential feedback and contributed to entries on: neoliberalism; place; and relationship anarchy.

John Winslade contributed the entries on discourse and neoliberalism.

Gipsy Hosking wrote the entry on ableism and contributed to the entry on disability.

Thanks also to David Newman and Manja Visschedijk for their early reading, suggestions and enthusiasm for this project.

And three broader acknowledgements:

To Michael White, whose political commitments, brilliance and hard work generated new ways of understanding and forms of practice that fill many of the pages of this book.

To David Epston, who not only co-founded narrative therapy, but whose creativity and generosity also provided the precursors for collective narrative practice.

And to Cheryl White whose joyful, intelligent politics has made possible this project and so many others.

a

6

'A stick on its own is easily broken but a bundle will not break'

A proverb from Malawi which was used as part of the first collective externalising conversation by CARE Counsellors interviewing the characters of HIV/AIDS and CARE (Community Action Renders Enablement). The metaphor was used as part of a ritual in which the character CARE first asked participants to break a single stick:

> Slowly Mr/Mrs CARE picks up a stick, a piece of wood from nearby trees known by the local people to be magical. With the stick in hand, Mr/Mrs CARE turns and offers it to the nearest person and asks them to use their strength to break it. The first person cannot, and so the stick is passed slowly and quietly. Finally it cracks and breaks in two.
>
> *One stick on its own is easily broken.*
> Removing the broken stick, Mr/Mrs CARE turns and picks up a bundle of sticks, also from the magic trees, but this time bound together by twine. The villagers are invited to try to break the bundle. This time they cannot.
>
> *One stick on its own is easily broken, but, if you put sticks in a bundle, that bundle becomes very strong, so strong that you cannot break it. A spirit on its own can be easily broken. But bundled together we will not break. That is our power and our strength. Pang'ono pang'ono ndi mtolo – little by little we must make a bundle.*
> (Sliep & CARE Counsellors, 1996, p. 145)

A literal 'bundle of sticks' was given by CARE Counsellors to the Power to our Journeys Group (Sue, Mem & Veronika, 1999) and the metaphor has since been used by many different communities.

Ableism

This entry was written by Gipsy Hosking

Ableism involves the assumption that the abled body is the normal or natural body (normal of form and function). As a consequence of this assumption other bodies – so called disabled bodies – become by definition abnormal, inferior, devalued. Ableism can be experienced by people with physical impairments, intellectual disabilities, mental illness, chronic illness and those who are neurodivergent. The flip side of the marginalisation that is a product of ableism, is able-bodied privilege – privilege experienced by those deemed to have 'able' / 'normal' bodies.

[See DISABILITY]

Abolition democracy

> For authentic democracy to emerge, [Angela] Davis argues, *abolition democracy* must be enacted – the abolition of institutions that advance the dominance of any one group over any other. Abolition democracy, then, is the democracy that is to come. (Mendieta in Davis, 2005, p. 16)

[See PRISON ABOLITIONISM]

Absent but implicit

A concept/practice described by Michael White – drawing on the work of Bateson (1980) and Derrida (1978) – that emphasises how all expressions of experience (emotion/meaning/action) are relational, they depend on contrasts and discernments:

> Any expression in life requires an act of discernment … We cannot give expression to our experience unless we can distinguish it in relation to something else … we can only do this through contrasts … A person would not be experiencing despair if they had no familiarity with hope … if people did not have experiences of hope then they would have resignation, not despair, they would be resigned to these negative circumstances of their life. (White, n.d.-a)
>
> Let me offer an example: Let's say a person consults me about 'despair'. I will first want to understand as best I can their experience of this despair, and how it manifests itself in their lives. I will also want to understand as best I can the contexts of this despair, which can include socioeconomic conditions

> and the power relations of local culture. These contexts can be subsequently foregrounded and addressed in a variety of ways. But I will also be interested in what it is that this despair speaks to, or what it is a testimony to, in terms of the absent but implicit – in how the person came to identify and to represent their experience in this way, in the circumstances or conditions that made it possible for them to discern despair. (White, 2000a, p. 37)

If narrative practitioners can carefully unpack expressions of sorrow, despair, failure, and so on, this can make visible what these expressions have been contrasted against, often treasured values that have been violated. This concept/practice can therefore provide renewed options for responding to those who are suffering. This is true not only in individual or family conversations but also in relation to work with communities:

> i. inferiority and inadequacy might be newly appreciated as evidence of defiance and non-conformity;
>
> ii. failure might be newly understood to be a reflection of independent mindedness;
>
> iii. damage and disability might be taken to denote special insider knowledges of tyranny that contribute to a uniquely-abled life;
>
> iv. culpability for what one has been through might be newly perceived to be expressions of precious survival skills;
>
> v. dependence might be newly acknowledged as a commitment to the ethic of collaborative action;
>
> vi. neediness might be newly recognised to reflect a special consciousness of injustices, including those associated with the politics of disadvantage;
>
> vii. passivity might be newly appreciated as an unwillingness to visit on the lives of others what has been visited upon one's own life;
>
> viii. weakness might be newly understood to reflect compassion and open mindedness, and so on. (White, 2003, p. 35)

[See DOUBLE LISTENING; EXPRESSIONS OF EXPERIENCE]

Accomplices (and recruits of domination)

A way of understanding men who perpetrate abuse that emphasises individual men's responsibility for their actions as well as men's collective responsibilities:

> The assumption that men who perpetrate abuse are not the originators of these techniques of power or the authors of these constructions of identity and gender leads to a perspective that they are accomplices to the projects of domination that are shaped by these discourses. This assumption also leads to the perspective that these men are recruits, and that as recruits, they have undergone an apprenticeship in these abusive ways of being.
>
> This assumption that these men are accomplices and recruits does not diminish the acknowledgment that they are individually responsible for the acts of tyranny that they have perpetrated on the lives of others. But it does support the conclusion that it is the responsibility of men (as a community) to:
>
> - Address abuse.
> - Develop an exposé of the discourses of men's culture.
> - Make reparation.
> - Develop ways of being in the world and in relationships to others that are not exploitative and that are nonabusive. (White, 2011a, p. 100)

The term accomplice is also sometimes used as an alternative to, and complication of, the concept of 'allies':

> For social justice advocates who use the term accomplice, they often see the site of focus as the main difference between the work of an ally and that of an accomplice. An ally will mostly engage in activism by standing with an individual or group in a marginalized community. An accomplice will focus more on dismantling the structures that oppress that individual or group – and such work will be directed by the stakeholders in the marginalized group. Simply, ally work focuses on individuals, and accomplice work focuses on the structures of decision-making agency. (Clemens, 2017)

Accountability processes

The Just Therapy Team of the Family Centre of Lower Hutt, Aotearoa New Zealand, has written about their efforts to create accountability processes through the development of partnerships between dominant and marginalised groups (Kiwi Tamasese, Charles Waldegrave, Flora Tuhaka, & Warihi Campbell, 1998).

Considerations of accountability processes are also relevant when working with those who have perpetrated abuse:

> I have discussed the emphasis that can be given to processes of accountability in work with men who have perpetrated abuse (White 1995a). In this work, attention is given to the exploration of knowledges about alternative ways of being for men, and to the development of specific proposals for action that are informed by these knowledges. Once established, feedback on these proposals is solicited from women and from children. This provides some check on the unwitting reproduction of those men's ways of being in the world that are oppressive to others. I have also discussed the development of processes of accountability in my work with women who have been subject to abuse by men (White 1995a). This accountability is often facilitated by engaging other women as consultants to the therapeutic conversations. Special attention can be given to the review of any developments in therapy that might be reproducing of the power relations of gender. These processes of accountability are decentring of the knowledges and of the consciousness of the therapist in regard to the many considerations of the real effects of this work. (White, 1997, p. 204)

[See PARTNERSHIPS ACROSS GENDER AND CULTURE]

Add your own entry

This is a space in which in to add your own favourite political concept, principle or commitment:

Agent-deletion

A method discussed by Julia P. Stanley (1975) of erasing responsibility in linguistic structures, especially characteristic of professional languages ... 'In other contexts the agent is deleted in order to protect agents responsible for the action [e.g. "Mary was sexually abused as a young child" obscures the fact that she was abused *by her father*].' (Julia P. Stanley 1974) (Kramarae & Treichler, 1985, p. 38)

[See DISEMBODIED SPEECH]

Alternative texts

Written documentation that testifies to the insider knowledge, skills and hopes of the person concerned and that acts as a counterpoint to the psychiatric file:

> It has been proposed elsewhere that the libraries of psychiatric hospitals be obliged to include … alternative texts … and that these be placed alongside the more formal psychiatric texts. These alternative texts just might be more helpful to people who are struggling with troublesome voices and visions than the standard texts. (Brigitte, Sue, Mem & Veronika, 1997, p. 210)

[See CERTIFICATES; DOCUMENTS OF IDENTITY; INSIDER KNOWLEDGE]

'An activist in my own mind'

Sue Ridgway's description of what it is like to hear and respond to hostile voices that are often shaped by patriarchy, sexism and authoritarianism. Sue was one of the inaugural members of the Power to Our Journeys Group. Prior to receiving a diagnosis of schizophrenia, she had been involved in various forms of activism shaped by lesbian feminist environmental politics.

[See POWER TO OUR JOURNEYS]

Anti-Anorexia/Bulimia league

> Through the process of reclaiming their lives back from anorexia and bulimia, League members refused to accept the popular misconception that they alone were responsible for their so-called eating disorders. League members began to make a crucial shift in their identities from group therapy patients to community activists and experienced consultants. In helping at the level of community, they assisted other women and families and, in turn, helped themselves. The purpose of the Vancouver League was also to traverse the questionable ideological and fiscal gaps that lay within a traditional treatment terrain of mental health. (Madigan, 2019, p. 187)

[See ARCHIVE]

'I feel apprehensive whenever I first sit down with a family'

Michael White

Apprehension A form of concern positively evaluated by Michael White as a reflection of modesty on the part of therapists/professionals:

> … it's important the apprehension is not paralysing, but … apprehension gets disqualified, it gets read in very pathologising ways, and it's read as a lack of confidence, or a lack of skills … because of that we have a field that is so through and through immodest, totally immodest and so people believe that they can ask any questions of anybody without even asking permission if they can ask questions about those areas, or without checking with people about how conversations are going with them, you know, practices in this field are so immodest. So, I think it's good for us to be thinking about how we can positively evaluate apprehension and look at what it speaks to, you know, what it's a reflection of in terms of really, really important things … (White, n.d.-a)

> I feel apprehensive whenever I first sit down with a family and I've been doing this work for many, many years, and I think if I don't ever feel a fraction apprehensive, I don't mean paralysing apprehension, but if I don't experience that apprehension then I think I should quit. Cause then I'll really think that I've stepped into that immodesty that's named less kindly as arrogance. (White, n.d.-a)

Archive

David Epston, one of the founders of narrative therapy, originally worked as an anthropologist and studied community development before becoming a social worker. In the 1980s, he began to circulate the knowledges of those who consulted him in therapy to others who were experiencing similar difficulties. He collected client 'wisdoms', and what he referred to as client 'expert knowledge', into archives (Epston, 2001). These archives contained audiotapes, letters, and artwork that represented 'a rich supply of solutions to an assortment of longstanding problems such as temper taming, night fears, school refusing, asthma … anorexia and bulimia' (Madigan & Epston, 1995, p. 263). Gradually, David Epston began to create networks of clients which he called 'leagues' so that they could provide consultation, information and support to each other. The best-known example of such a league is the Anti-Anorexia/Anti-Bulimia League (Epston & Maisel, 2009; Grieves, 1997; Lock, Epston & Maisel 2004; Lock, Epston, Maisel & de Faria, 2005; Madigan, 2019; Maisel, Epston & Borden, 2004). This approach to linking groups of clients in order to share 'solution knowledges' came to be known as generating 'communities of concern' (Madigan & Epston, 1995; Madigan, 2011). Employing then new technologies, these communities of concern first used fax machines to send messages around the world. This was followed by online leagues to respond to various issues, including the 'Archive of resistance: Anti-anorexia/anti-bulimia' (www.narrativeapproaches.com). The development of archives and leagues were key precedents for what is now referred to as collective narrative practice.

Aromantic

Perhaps the most insidious assumptions around gender, sexuality, and relationships currently are that people inevitably have a gender, and sexual and romantic attractions. The sexual and romantic imperatives make life very hard indeed for asexual people who do not experience sexual attraction and aromantic people who do not experience romantic attraction. (Barker, 2018, p. 51)

Asexuality

Asexuality, or ace, is an umbrella term for people who do not experience sexual attraction. The concept of an asexual spectrum also includes those who have little sexual attraction or rarely experience it (grey-A people), and those who experience it only under certain conditions, such as when they have a strong emotional connection (demisexual people). The notion of a spectrum opens up our understanding of sexual attraction to range from none at all, to very high, without any place on that spectrum being indicative of a 'disorder' or 'pathology'... Asexual people may be celibate or not. Some are averse to sex, whereas some are willing to have it for other reasons than sexual attraction, for example to give a partner sexual pleasure, or in return for other forms of pleasure. Some may have solo sex, others do not. Some experience their asexuality as fluid, others as fixed. Many asexual people want romantic relationships, whereas aromantic people do not. (Barker, 2018 pp. 32–33)

[See AROMANTIC]

Assigned sex

This entry was written by Tiffany Sostar

Assigned sex is the sex one is assigned at birth, typically based on birth genitalia. In western societies, one is usually assigned one of two primary binary sexes: male or female, and these sexes are assumed to correlate to two binary genders: man or woman. This perpetuates the false understanding that there are only two sexes, thereby erasing intersex individuals, and the false understanding that there are only two genders, contributing to the erasure and pathologisation of non-binary and transgender individuals. Assigned sex and assumed gender work together to uphold cisnormativity.

[See CISGENDER/CIS; INTERSEX; NON-BINARY; TRANSGENDER]

Audiences

In the 1980s, along with my friend and colleague David Epston, I began to actively engage audiences in my work with families. This was partly inspired by our observations of the extent to which many of the children we met with spontaneously recruited audiences to the preferred developments of their lives. For example, in the context of our meetings with families, children would be awarded certificates that acknowledged significant achievements in their effort to reclaim their lives from troublesome problems. Invariably these children would show this certificate to others – perhaps to their siblings, cousins, friends, or peers at school. This usually had the effect of prompting questions from the 'audience', which provided an opportunity for these children to give an account of the feats signified by the certificate and at times to actually demonstrate their prowess. These questions and responses from the 'audience' were clearly influential in acknowledging the preferred developments in these children's lives, in contributing to the endurance of these developments, and in extending them. (White, 2007, p. 178)

[See OUTSIDER WITNESS]

Autonomy as an attitude of permanent critique

Lois McNay:

> For Foucault, the aim of … autonomy is not to achieve a state of impersonal moral transcendence, but rather to refuse to submit to the government of individualisation by constantly interrogating what seems to be the natural and inevitable in one's own identity:
>
> > *We must try to proceed with the analysis of ourselves as beings who are historically determined …* (Foucault, 1984a: 43)
>
> Foucault's notion of autonomy as an attitude of permanent critique contrasts with the naturalized notion of autonomy … (McNay, 1992, p. 104)

Avoiding complicity with dominant culture

Some awareness of the extent to which the culture of therapy reproduces the dominant culture can assist us in our search for a therapeutic posture that is not wholly complicit with this. This posture can include a determination to:

> a) assist persons to explore the real effects, on their lives and relationships, of some of the privileged knowledges and practices of power of dominant culture;
>
> b) encourage persons to honour and embrace their resistance to the incitements of these dominant knowledges and practices of power;
>
> c) privilege alternative knowledges and frames of meaning that are associated with this resistance;
>
> d) establish the sort of structures of accountability that might expose the real and the potential abuses of power in the practices of therapy;
>
> e) subvert the hierarchies of knowledge of the culture of psychotherapy;
>
> f) acknowledge one's location in the social world – gender, race, class, ethnicity, sexual preference, etc. – and the various implications of this location;
>
> g) acknowledge the contribution of therapeutic interaction in the shaping of one's own life;
>
> h) consistently interview families about their experience of therapy, and about their interpretations of our motives and of our conduct;
>
> i) recognise and respect the fact that it is not possible for the therapeutic context to be an entirely egalitarian context, but to strive to render it more so. (White, 1998, pp. 228–229)

b

d

Becoming squarehead

One way of describing an ongoing process of rewriting and understanding middle-class life through the experiences of working-class people:

> Working in prisons has meant coming in contact with communities that are not my own. To find myself teaching a welfare/sociology class to long-termers in a maximum security prison was to find myself transported into a culture very different from the white middle-class world to which I am accustomed. One morning I naively asked the group what they would have called me had we met as children. Without a moment's hesitation, and with a dead-pan expression, one guy replied, 'A squarehead'. Unfazed, I asked what this meant and with a large grin he explained, 'A stuck-up poof who can't fuck'. My lessons had begun. Far from sounding like an insult (or a challenge to explore issues of sexuality or homophobia), it seemed a generous, if rather blunt, invitation to explore our differences and my privilege.
>
> At this stage, in hysterics and with laughter filling the room, I managed to articulate that I would have thought of them as 'westies' (from the western suburbs), but that I wouldn't have dared call them this to their faces, as I would have been terrified of being beaten up by the violent, ugly and stupid young men that I believed they were!
>
> Believe it or not, this was the beginning of ongoing attempts to build partnerships across a class divide. Their naming of my middle-class experience challenged me to explore and articulate what it means to be middle-class. It was the beginning of an ongoing process of rewriting and understanding my life through the experiences of working-class people. It is this process that I refer to as 'becoming squarehead'.
>
> … One of the first things that was absolutely clear was that they were much more familiar with the term 'westie' than I was with the term 'squarehead'. To be middle-class means that one's culture is rarely the 'object' of analysis. (Denborough, 1995a, p. 113)

[See CLASS RELATIONS (MENTAL HEALTH)]

'relationships between generations continually re-make culture; they always have, and they always will.'

Beyond the tradition/ modernity divide

In community projects involving different generations of refugees/migrants, collective narrative practices are sometimes used to try to provide a way beyond the 'tradition/ modernity' divide (Nicholls & North, 2001, p. 4).

Too often, when tradition and modernity are described or experienced as separate, this contributes to a divide between generations – the older generation comes to represent 'tradition' in contrast with the younger generation representing 'modernity'. By eliciting 'modern' skills and initiatives and then tracing the social and cultural histories of these, principles come to be experienced as both tradition and modernity. Significantly, this can provide a renewed 'faith in culture':

> 'Faith in culture brings psychological well-being. You believe that your culture has resources to solve your problems. When you come here [Australia] that resource becomes more complex' (Participant interview in Westoby, 2009, p. 51).

As this Sudanese refugee explains, 'faith in culture' is precious. By eliciting 'modern' or current initiatives and skills and then tracing the social histories of these, it becomes possible to re-associate current social actions and initiatives with 'culture'. In doing so, it also becomes clearer that 'culture is always in progress' (Bruner, 2005, p. 161) and that the relationships between generations continually re-make culture; they always have, and they always will. (Denborough, 2010a, p. 22)

Binary thinking

Part of a system of understanding that embeds and naturalises hierarchies and oppositions (see Derrida, 1967/2016).

> Binary oppositions … refer to a practice that runs through western thought of arranging conceptual/theoretical systems in opposed, contrasting pairs. The idea is that *good*, for example, can be understood only in contrast with *bad*, *light* by contrast with *dark*. Characterising these contrasts as *bipolar* represents the opposed terms as radically separate from one another, not as points on a continuum. This arrangement might appear to be a perfectly neutral way of classifying attributes of the world, both physical and human. But feminist critiques contest the neutrality, showing that the pairs mark not merely descriptive but also evaluative contrasts, which are enlisted to condemn one 'side' while promoting and celebrating the other. The male/female polarity is no exception. (Code, 2000, p. 44)

[See ABSENT BUT IMPLICIT; DECONSTRUCTION]

Biphobia

Dislike of or prejudice against bisexual people.

> Biphobia … is direct negative attitudes and treatment of bi* people. It's one specific result of monosexism. So here we can think about the many negative attitudes and behaviours specifically aimed against bis*. For example, when people refuse to date bisexuals*, when bis* are represented in stereotypical ways in the media, when bi* women become the target of sexual violence (because they're perceived as particularly sexy sexual objects), when bi* people are discriminated at their jobs because of their bisexuality (for example, because they're perceived as unreliable, flaky, unable to handle responsibility or commit to their job), and, yes – when bi* people are treated badly by L, G, and T communities. (Eisner, 2013)

[See MONOSEXISM]

Bisexuality/ pansexuality

There are a number of terms for people who are attracted to more than one gender, or for whom the gender of the person they are attracted to is irrelevant, or not particularly relevant. Some prefer the word bisexual (with the 'bi' standing for attraction to 'the same gender as me' and 'different genders to me'). Others prefer 'pansexual' to capture the irrelevance of a person's gender, or queer to challenge the whole idea of binary gender and sexuality (see Barker and Scheele, 2016). 'Bisexuality' is often used as the umbrella term for these kinds of identities and experiences given it is the term recognised by official bodies as part of LGBT. (Barker, 2018, p. 34)

Black feminism

Joan Morgan:

> White girls don't call their men 'brothers' and that made their struggle enviably simpler than mine. Racism and the will to survive it creates a sense of intra-racial loyalty that makes it impossible for black women to turn our backs on black men – even in their ugliest and most sexist of moments. I needed a feminism that would allow us to continue loving ourselves and the brothers who hurt us without letting race loyalty buy us early tombstones. (Morgan, 2000, p. 36)

Border imperialism

A concept articulated by Harsha Walia:

> For the past several years, Indigenous organizations in Australia have been issuing 'Original Passports' to asylum seekers who have been detained or denied legal status by the Australian government. Most recently … passports were issued to two detained Tamil asylum seekers. During the ceremony, Ray Jackson of the Indigenous Social Justice Association said, 'The Australian Government must stop imprisoning Indigenous people, and they must stop imprisoning asylum seekers. I am proud to welcome people in need into our community.' Indigenous elder Robbie Thorpe commented, 'The Australian Government has no legitimate right to grant or refuse entry to anyone in this country, let alone lock up people fleeing war and persecution.'
>
> Such moments of solidarity between Indigenous people and migrants represent not only growing networks of understanding and alliance between marginalized communities, but also a fundamental challenge to the authority of settler-colonial governments and the sovereignty of Western statehood. Western governance and statehood is constituted through multiple modes, including the primacy of the border that delineates and reproduces territorial, political, economic, cultural, and social control … Constantly being redefined, borders represent a regime of practices, institutions, discourses, and systems that I define as border imperialism. (Walia, 2013, pp. 37–38)

Burnout

Burnout is an idea that is very individually structured, as if there is something about us personally that makes us measure up to this work or not. I think that the prevalence of what is being called burnout says more about our society than it says about individual workers. I do not deny that as therapists and community workers we can be harmed and experience pain in our work, even to the extent of needing to leave the work, or take time out. What I am contesting is the prescriptive, individualised accusations burnout levies against workers which invisibilise and obscure the contexts of social injustice we work in, and blame clients for the harms we experience. (Reynolds, 2011, pp. 28–29).

Non-individualist ways of sustaining workers and preventing what is sometimes called 'burnout' are discussed in Reynolds (2011), White (1997) and Denborough (2018).

C

Certificate

A form of alternative text to acknowledge the efforts of people to reclaim their lives from the effects of problems and/or to resist dominant cultural prescriptions:

> *Escape from Guilt Certificate*
>
> This certificate is awarded to ____________ in recognition of her victory over guilt. Now that guilt doesn't have such a priority in her life, she is able to give herself a priority in her own life. Now that she is not guilt's person, she is free to be her own person.
>
> This certificate will serve to remind ____________ and others, that she has resigned from the position of super-responsibility in the lives of others, and that she is no longer vulnerable to invitations from others to have their life for them and to put her life to one side.
>
> Awarded on the _________ day of ______
>
> Signed:
>
> Michael White (White & Epston, 1990, p. 200)

[See ALTERNATIVE TEXT]

Charter (draft) of Storytelling Rights

A way of conceptualising some of the principles and ethics of narrative practice, developed by David Denborough to support the work of Human Rights organisations in Palestine and Rwanda. It will forever remain as a draft as it may require adaptations in differing cultural contexts. It is written in a style echoing the language of the United Nations Declaration of Human Rights. See: https://dulwichcentre.com.au/narrative-justice-and-human-rights/

- Article 1: Everyone has the right to define their experiences and problems in their own words and terms.

- Article 2: Everyone has the right for their life to be understood in the context of what they have been through and in the context of their relationships with others.

- Article 3: Everyone has the right to invite others who are important to them to be involved in the process of reclaiming their life from the effects of trauma.

- Article 4: Everyone has the right to be free from having problems caused by trauma and injustice located inside them, internally, as if there is some deficit in them. The person is not the problem, the problem is the problem.

- Article 5: Everyone has the right for their responses to trauma to be acknowledged. No one is a passive recipient of trauma. People always respond. People always protest injustice.

- Article 6: Everyone has the right to have their skills and knowledges of survival respected, honoured and acknowledged.

- Article 7: Everyone has the right to know and experience that what they have learnt through hardship can make a contribution to others in similar situations. (Denborough, 2014, p. 9).

For discussion of Michel Foucault's conceptions of rights and rights discourse beyond liberalism, see Golder (2015).

[See STORYTELLING RIGHTS]

Checking for collusion

One of the dimensions of critical thinking described by Mary Heath (2012):

> There are … situations in which we may feel pulled to think or act in ways which conflict with our ethical standards. It helps to check whether we are colluding in unethical conduct or thinking because doing so feels familiar or comfortable or because it is in our interest in some way by examining our thoughts and feelings. We can ask questions such as: How am I feeling about this claim? What am I thinking about this claim? Am I more likely to accept this claim without critical examination because I'm inclined to agree with it? How does accepting this claim reinforce my privilege? How does this claim reinforce the ways I may have internalised oppressive messages about people like me or 'them'? Am I pulled to collude with the claim in order to remain comfortable, or to resist self-examination? Would doing so be ethical for me? (p. 17)

Checklist of social and psychological resistance

Initially developed to honour the social and psychological resistance of communities whose experiences of hardship were being viewed in pathologising ways through the lens of PTSD checklists (Denborough, 2008), these checklists are now being used in diverse contexts, including as a research method (Hoosain, 2013).

Cisgender/ cis

> Cisgender, or cis, is an umbrella term for those who remain in the gender that was assumed when they were born. The term was coined because it is marginalising only to label those who differ from a cultural norm: trans people in the case of gender status. The cis prefix means 'on this side of', as opposed to trans which means 'across from'. As with heterosexuality, monogamy, or whiteness, naming cis-ness, enables us to open it up for discussion in terms of its impact on an individual and their social level. (Barker, 2018, p. 24)

[See ASSIGNED SEX; NON-BINARY; TRANSGENDER]

Class relations (mental health)

Mickey de Valda (2003), a key member of the Hearing Voices Network in Manchester, UK, eloquently described the significance of the influence of class in mental health:

> I am particularly interested in how issues of class influence mental health. I believe that working-class people are especially at risk in their interactions with mental health professionals. If you approach a psychiatric service without a given amount of knowledge and education you are incredibly vulnerable. In my experience, working-class people are a little more likely to accept their label and live it, act it out and become the schizophrenic that they are told that they are.
>
> If you consider the plight of the sub-working-class voice-hearers, the risk is more extreme. Those within prisons for instance, who ask for the help of a psychiatrist, are almost always drug abusers and with histories of trauma. They seem almost guaranteed to acquire a psychiatric label before too long … I know the effects of a lack of education. In fact, at times I can almost feel incapacitated with ignorance. Recently I bought one of the study guides for high school students on psychology. It was in an Oxfam shop. When I read through this I couldn't get over the fact that there must be so many young people studying at that level, 17-18 years old with the most extraordinary knowledge. I remember when I used to go to social security and the eighteen-year-old behind the counter would tell me what we should have done with our money the previous week and how we should have made it last. This caused resentment at the time. But now, when I think about the eighteen-year-olds who are so well educated, like my niece who is studying law, it can take my breath away. I am truly glad these young people have these opportunities. It's just that many working-class people who haven't had these chances can literally feel overcome by the sensation of ignorance. I can almost tremble if I think about it.

Class relations (mental health)

(continued)

> Most health professionals live a middle-class life and this has real effects for those of us using the services. For instance, it is very common for me to feel confused when professional people tell me positive things about my skills or abilities. While they are trying to be supportive, it is difficult for me to separate what they are saying from the many instances of positive reinforcement I was offered when in the psychiatric system. False positive statements from professional middle-class people can really limit the possibility for honest communication. At times it can become difficult for me to discern whether I actually am doing something significant or whether the person is just offering positive reinforcement. (de Valda, 2003, pp. 16–17)

[See BECOMING SQUAREHEAD]

Collective accountability

Vikki Reynolds grounds her approach to supervision in teams on explorations of collective accountability and collective ethics:

> Collective accountability requires that we are responsible for more than our personal actions. For example, if a client is disrespected in our workspace, we are all collectively accountable for that affront to dignity, and cannot just find which staff member to blame. We are required to make repair collectively as well. For example, if there is a person on the team who acts as a bully, we have a collective responsibility to address that situation. If we do not, because of our own concerns for our comfort or even safety, we leave clients vulnerable to known risks, which is unethical. (Reynolds, 2013, p. 9)

[See COLLECTIVE ETHICS]

Collective documents

Collective documents can be used to start a process of mutual contribution between groups and communities. They often describe the skills and knowledges that people are engaging with to deal with hard times and are constructed in ways that seek to generate communitas. (See Denborough, 2008)

[See COLLECTIVE NARRATIVE PRACTICE; COMMUNITAS; ENABLING CONTRIBUTION]

Collective ethics

Collective ethics are those important points of connection that weave us together as therapists and community workers. In most of our work these collective ethics go unnamed, but they are the basis for the solidarity that brought us together and can hold us together. I have found it useful to map out collective ethics within teams of workers to invite a collective commitment to these ethics and create shared meanings. Naming collectively held ethics can invite rich critique, and clearer agreements. (Reynolds, 2011, p. 30)

Collective externalising conversations

A particularly popular and accessible form of collective narrative practice developed by Yvonne Sliep when working in partnership with the CARE Counsellors of Malawi (Sliep & CARE Counsellors, 1996). In responding to the HIV/AIDS epidemic in rural Malawi, local health workers applied the narrative concept of 'externalising problems' (see Roth & Epston, 1996) in theatrical ways. Community members were invited to interview health workers who played the roles of 'Mr AIDS' and 'Mrs CARE' (representing Community Action Renders Enablement). Yvonne Sliep has gone on further to develop forms of narrative theatre (2005), while Aboriginal health worker, Barbara Wingard, has developed her own forms of collective externalising conversations in response to diabetes ('sugar') grief, and lateral violence (Wingard, 1996a, 1996b, 2010). Others have taken this approach into school contexts (McMenamin, 1999).

[See A STICK ON ITS OWN IS EASILY BROKEN; EXTERNALISING]

Collective narrative practice

A term used to describe the use of narrative practices outside the therapy room and in particular to link individuals, groups and/or communities (Denborough, 2008). Collective narrative practice is characterised by these ten themes:

1. As we listen to and seek to respond to the stories that individuals and groups share with us, we can conceive of these stories as representing not only personal experience, but also the effects of broader social issues.

2. No matter the degree of hardship, trauma or desolation, individuals, groups and communities will be *responding* to the situations they are in. There will be initiatives they are taking to try to reduce or redress the harm and/or to care for and protect others.

3. Rather than bringing our own initiatives to work within these communities, our role instead can be to create contexts in which people's own initiatives and healing knowledges are noticed and more richly described. This includes unearthing the skills, values, hopes and dreams that are implicit in people's responses to hardship, and the histories of these in the lives of individuals, cultures and communities.

4. Once these local initiatives, skills and values are acknowledged and documented, we can seek out a relevant audience to whom these will be resonant. This often involves other individuals/groups who are experiencing similar or related hardship – others who are affected by similar social issues.

5. It then becomes possible to enable those who are struggling with the effects of hardship to make meaningful contributions to the lives of others who are also struggling. In turn, this experience of making a contribution to others can lead to an increased sense of personal/collective agency.

6. It can be particularly significant when opportunities are created for two-way inter-generational contributions and inter-generational honouring. When it can be acknowledged that the skills and values of younger generations are carrying forth (in unique ways) the legacies of those from older generations, this can provide an antidote to the inter-generational dislocation that collective trauma often causes within communities.

7. People's responses to hardship and trauma are forms of local social action. By acknowledging these, by more richly describing them, and by creating an ever-increasing sense of personal/collective agency, this makes it possible for people's initiatives to become linked, and for further actions to be taken. These actions may be in relation to reclaiming their lives from effects of trauma/hardship and/or in relation to preventing further harm or injustice to themselves, their community, or others.

8. The generation and performance of 'local folk culture' can reinvigorate local healing knowledges and local social action. If rich descriptions of people's skills and knowledges in dealing with hardship can be transformed into local cultural mediums (written word, spoken word, song, film, dance, poetry, celebration) this makes many things possible. It can enable people to perform, witness and share within ceremonies of redefinition of identity (Myerhoff, 1982; White, 1999). This process of cultural creativity can also contribute to the sustenance and reinvigoration of the language of inner life (James, 1892). When engaged with collectively, this process can be sustaining of 'communitas' (Turner, 1969, 1979) and, importantly, of local social action (Adams & Horton, 1975).

9. Throughout this process, we can deliberately work for 'the invention of unity in diversity' (Freire, 1994, p. 157). There is a constant responsibility to ensure that the generation of connectedness or 'communitas' is not accompanied by the development of new forms of normalising judgement. These approaches seek to 'resurrect diversity in everyday life' (White, 2004a, p. vi) by consistently acknowledging the rich diversity of people's skills, knowledges, values and hopes for life.

10. Following Freire (Horton & Freire, 1990) we can approach this work with a broad view and a long timeline. Our task becomes to generate possibilities for those affected by social issues to make meaningful contributions to others also affected by these social issues, in ways that provide relief from the effects of trauma and that build both personal *and* collective agency. (Denborough, 2008, pp. 119–120)

[See COMMUNITAS]

'Collective ethics are those important points of connection that weave us together as therapists and community workers.'

Vikki Reynolds (2011, p. 30)

Communitas

Victor Turner preferred the Latin word 'communitas' to 'community' to describe a sense of shared unity among individuals who are going through the same experience (1969, p. 96). This concept informs collective narrative practice (Denborough, 2008):

> He [Victor Turner] observed experiences of 'communitas' in 'the workshop, village, lecture-room, theatre, almost anywhere' and described these experiences as essentially 'an unmediated relationship between historical, idiosyncratic, concrete individuals' (1979, p. 42). Significantly, he emphasised that experiences of communitas preserve 'individual distinctiveness – it is neither regression to infancy, nor it is emotional, nor it is "merging" in fantasy' (1979, p. 42). We have become interested in noticing the differing forms of 'communitas' that are generated in the work that we do. We are particularly interested in how experiences of communitas do not merge identities: 'the gifts of each person are alive to the full, along with those of every other person. Communitas liberates individuals from conformity to general norms' (Salamone, 2004, p. 98). We are also interested in how 'experiences of communitas do not depend on "in-group versus out-group" opposition' (Salamone, 2004, p. 98). (Denborough, 2008, p. 49)

The stories shared during the gathering ... articulated the healing knowledges of the community.

Community gatherings

In 1994 the first 'community gathering' informed by narrative ideas was held at Camp Coorong. This was a project initiated by the Aboriginal Health Council of South Australia in conjunction with Dulwich Centre, to respond to one of the recommendations of the inquiry into Aboriginal deaths in custody. Tim Agius and Michael White were instrumental in developing a form of community gathering that contributes to rich story development (see White, 2003). This involved extensive community consultations, the development of a number of themes to be discussed, and then the use of definitional ceremony structures and outsider witnesses during a residential gathering. The stories shared during the gathering, which articulated the healing knowledges of the community, were then documented in written form (Aboriginal Health Council of South Australia, 1995). This documentation was made available to all those present and also circulated more widely.

Following the success of the gathering at Camp Coorong, further narrative gatherings have been run for mental health consumers ('Speaking out', 1995), people with a HIV-positive diagnosis and workers in the HIV/AIDS sector ('Living positive lives', 2000), and in other Aboriginal communities both here in Australia (Denborough, 2002a) and overseas (Neighbouring Communities Project, 2007). Community songwriting (Denborough, 2002b) has also come to play a significant role in these gatherings. (Denborough, 2008, pp. 203–204)

Communities of concern

[See ARCHIVE; LEAGUE]

Concientization

Conscientization is a translation of the Portuguese term conscientização, which can also be translated as 'consciousness-raising' and 'critical consciousness'. The term was popularized by Brazilian educator, activist, and theorist Paulo Freire (1970). Within narrative practice, forms of externalising conversation, when they illuminate the social forces contributing to the creation and/or sustenance of problems, can contribute to conscientization.

[See CONSCIOUSNESS-RAISING; EXTERNALISING]

Conferences

The Dulwich Centre has attempted to host conferences in ways that are congruent with narrative practice politics and principles:

> Prior to the first of these events, we consulted widely in order to consider how we could take into account matters of culture, gender, class, sexual orientation, and other relations of power. While knowing that we would make many mistakes along the way, the following ideals were what we were aiming for:
>
> - to provide high quality presentations on the latest thinking and application of narrative ideas and to do so in ways that enable people of differing experience to be both engaged and challenged
> - to enable people of different cultures, countries, genders, ages, class backgrounds, physical abilities, and sexual identities to come together, enjoy each other's company, and have a sense that the conference program and processes include their perspectives, hopes, and ideas
> - to use the conference as a chance to acknowledge and come to terms with the history of the land on which it is held
> - to create an opportunity for participants to build a sense of connectedness and to contribute to the building of a community of ideas

Conferences

(continued)

- to provide the opportunity and support necessary for individuals and groups who have never presented before at conferences (and indeed may never have told their stories in front of an audience) to present the stories of their lives and their particular knowledges and skills in keynote addresses
- to create an atmosphere that is non-hierarchical, with no pronounced difference between presenters and participants
- to provide a forum for conversations that are expanding the field (not confirming it or simply reiterating what is already known)
- to de-centre the conference collective in both the lead-up and during the conference itself so that the focus remains on everyone's contributions to a community event. (White & Denborough, 2005, pp. 46–47).

Consciousness of local politics

As with any approach to working with persons who seek therapy, it is important that therapists do not make generalizations about situations, but keep in mind the specifics of every circumstance and think ahead to the likely consequences of particular courses of action. This argues for a certain level of 'consciousness' on the therapist's behalf. Further, lest the therapist inadvertently contribute to persons' experiences of oppression, this consciousness requires an appreciation of local politics – that is, politics at the level of relationships. (White & Epston, 1990, p. 49)

Consciousness-raising

Consciousness raising groups were a key element of the women's liberation movement.

> Feminists are made not born … Like all political positions one becomes a believer in feminist politics through choice and action … Revolutionary consciousness-raising emphasized the importance of learning about patriarchy as a system of domination, how it became institutionalized and how it is perpetuated and maintained. (hooks, 2000, p. 7)

> … consciousness-raising can be thought of as a feminist practice of the self … a practice of the self that involves not only self-transformation, but also social and political transformation. (McLaren, 2002, p. 155)

> Consciousness-raising assumes a relationship between the personal and the political … its advocates felt that the link between women's experience and sexist oppression was best articulated through consciousness-raising. Detractors of consciousness-raising, however, felt that consciousness-raising's strategy of self-transformation shifted the focus from the political to the personal … that it focused too much on the personal and individual and devolved into an issue of lifestyle rather than revolutionary social action. The well-known feminist slogan 'the personal is political' can be read in this way … However … many radical feminists … hoped that awareness of the impact of oppression on one's life would motivate women to change oppressive social and political structures. This reverses the sense of the phrase; the point is not to collapse the political into the personal or to make personal choices the end point of politics. Rather, the point is to understand the relationship between an individual's experience of oppression and oppressive political and social structures, with the aim of transforming them. This is clearly stated in one set of consciousness-raising philosophy in the phrase '*from* the personal *to* the political (emphasis added)'. The point of consciousness-raising was not to collapse the distinction between political and personal, nor to valorise individual lifestyle choices as political. Rather, the goal of consciousness-raising was to make women aware of the connection between their personal experience, especially with regard to their dissatisfaction with traditional social roles, and the sexist political and social institutions that perpetuate these traditional roles. (McLaren, 2002, pp. 158–9)

Consciousness-raising
(continued)

> The purpose of such consciousness-raising would not be to tell us who we are, but rather to free us from certain ways of understanding ourselves; that is, to tell us how we do not have to be and to tell us how we came to think of ourselves as we do. (Sawicki, 1991, p. 44)

[See CONSCIENTIZATION; DECONSTRUCTION]

Consulting your consultants

A key turn in the field of narrative therapy occurred when Michael White and David Epston began experimenting with consulting clients about their experiences and then sharing the results of these consultations with other clients:

> In this process, clients assume the role of expert in relation to the nature of their problems and their solutions. Such consultation has enabled Michael and David to:
>
> - Contribute to the endurance of change for the clients concerned.
> - Collect information and stories to add to their knowledge as therapists.
> - Investigate how this information can be directly passed onto and utilised by clients with similar problems. (White & Epston, 1986)

Co-production

> Co-production raises the bar for working with consumers [people who access mental health services], shifting from seeking involvement or participation after an agenda has already been set, to seeking consumer leadership from the outset so that consumers are engaged in the initial thinking and priority-setting processes.
>
> A co-production approach sees consumers involved in, or leading, defining the problem, designing and delivering the solution, and evaluating the outcome, either with professionals or independently. Co-production requires longer term engagement from professionals or clinicians, but leads to 'profound and sustainable change' (Spencer et al, 2013, p. 7). (Roper, Grey & Cadogan, 2018, p. 2)

Co-research

An alternative way of orientating to therapy devised by David Epston:

> I chose to orient myself around the co-research metaphor both because of its beguiling familiarity and because it radically departed from conventional clinical practice. It brought together the very respectable notion of research with the rather odd idea of the co-production of knowledge by sufferers and therapist. What made this possible, in the first instance, was a fairly thorough-going externalising conversation, one in which the problem was a problem for everyone – and here I included myself. Here's where I parted company from the disinterested ethnographer. This has led, and continually leads, to practices to discover a 'knowing' in such a fashion that all parties to it could make good use of it. Such knowledges are fiercely and unashamedly pragmatic. (Epston, 1999, pp. 141–142)

[See INSIDER KNOWLEDGE]

Counterstories

Counterstories come into being through a process of ongoing engagement with the narratives they resist. Many of them start small, like a seed in the crack of a sidewalk, but they are capable of displacing surprising chunks of concrete as they grow.

How much of the sidewalk a counterstory displaces is a function of the degree to which it resists the master narrative. Because the purpose of a counterstory is to repair an identity, the resistance it offers must, at a minimum, aim to dislodge some portion of the master narrative from a person's understanding of who she herself is, even if there is no attempt to push the counterstory into the broader community. (Nelson, 2001, p. 169)

Collective counterstories are sometimes documented and circulated within community projects, such as the *Yia Marra* stories:

> Richly told 'counter stories' (Nelson, 2001) from rural and remote Aboriginal communities have the potential to alter the perceptions of mainstream Australia. They have the potential to dislodge the pathologising and problem-saturated accounts that are pervasive within the media and popular imagination. This can have significant implications, as Nelson describes:
>
> *If the dominant group, moved by the counterstory, sees subordinates as developed moral agents, it may be less inclined to deprive them of the opportunity to enjoy valuable roles, relationships and goods.* (2001, p. 7)
>
> The Yia Marra stories have already been shared within international forums and with politicians. They are stories that speak both inward and outward. They can be seen as 'narrative acts of insubordination' (Nelson, 2001, p. 8). (Denborough, Wingard, & White, 2009, p. 27)

[See SUBORDINATE STORYLINE; SECOND STORY]

'Culture is constructed as the more powerful and the less powerful segments of society contend for positions of power and privilege between themselves.'

Makungu Akinyela

Culture

... culture is constructed as the more powerful and the less powerful segments of society contend for positions of power and privilege between themselves. This means that any given culture is actually a complex of contentious and complimentary interactions between asymmetrical class, gender, religious, language, sexual and other social groups. Viewed from this perspective, culture is in a constant dialectical process of construction and reconstruction. This notion suggests that there is really no homogenous national culture so much as systems of contending social groups within national or ethnic communities. It is the contention and complementarity between these groups that continually produces and reproduces culture.

It is the tendency of culture to adapt from and adapt to outside influences as well as to influence other cultures. Culture is constructed in the constant process of dynamic change. The resulting material manifestations of cultural phenomena – for example the artistic, social, and political expressions of groups and individuals – are behaviours of resistance and survival that assist and motivate cultural actors to make sense of and give meaning to their collective existence. (Akinyela, 2002, p. 34)

d

b

Damage-centred research (a moratorium)

Indigenous academic Eve Tuck, in her influential letter, *'Suspending Damage: A Letter to Communities'* (2009), calls for a moratorium on 'damage-centered' research in First Nations communities – including research that intends to document peoples' pain and brokenness to hold those in power accountable for their oppression:

> Is it time for our communities to call a moratorium on damage-centered research? How might this moratorium be useful to us?
>
> I humbly submit that the time has come for our communities to refuse to be complicit in our further categorization as only damaged, as only broken. In many communities, such a moratorium is already under way, and both 'insider' and 'outsider' researchers who employ a damage framework are being turned away at the gate. (Tuck, 2009, p. 422)

De-centred and yet influential

A political orientation that involves the practitioner centring the insider (local) knowledge and expertise of the person consulting them and refusing to interpret the lives of others, while upholding responsibilities to:

- render visible certain aspects of their taken-for-granted ways of being and thinking, to expand their consciousness of their biases.
- acknowledge their location in the social world, and the privileges and the limits of understanding that are associated with this location.
- acknowledge the assumptions and purposes that are associated with those metaphors that guide their work.
- honour the unique understandings and experiences of life that pertain to their location in the world of gender, race, class, culture.
- scaffold conversations to make it possible for people to incrementally and progressively distance themselves from the known and familiar toward what it might be possible for them to know and to do.
- ensure people are not vulnerable to an experience of re-traumatisation in the context of speaking about what they have been through. (see White, 2011b)

[See INSIDER KNOWLEDGE]

Decolonisation

> The very process of deliberately constructing a post-colonial therapy … will generate something new. The process of decolonization always does. The result of decolonization is not to return to the state that existed prior to colonization – that is never possible. The task is to free ourselves from the assumptions of the dominant culture, to place ourselves into the flow of our own culture and self-determined history in order to create our own ways of healing for New Afrikan families. (Akinyela, 2002, p. 40)

[See DECOLONISING IDENTITY STORIES; DECOLONISATION IS NOT A METAPHOR]

Decolonisation is not a metaphor

Decolonization brings about the repatriation of Indigenous land and life; it is not a metaphor for other things we want to do to improve our societies and schools. The easy adoption of decolonizing discourse by educational advocacy and scholarship, evidenced by the increasing number of calls to 'decolonize our schools', or use 'decolonizing methods', or, 'decolonize student thinking', turns decolonization into a metaphor. As important as their goals may be, social justice, critical methodologies, or approaches that decenter settler perspectives have objectives that may be incommensurable with decolonization. (Tuck & Yang, 2012, p. 1)

[See DECOLONISATION; DECOLONIZING IDENTITY STORIES]

Decolonising identity stories

Narrative practice enables people to explore their identity as a story. We consider negative identity conclusions and place these within the broader context of societal discourses (White, 2002a). This allows us to explore ideas of 'normality' and to make visible what norms we are often measuring ourselves against. In an Aboriginal context, identity conclusions may be impacted on by the experience of racism and, furthermore, ideas of normality are racially-based. As Rigney (1999) discusses, there is no process or structure within Australian society that is not impacted by racism. Through exploring identity as a story, and by acknowledging the impact of racism and the intersections of oppression and disadvantage that may be influencing the labels or diagnoses that Aboriginal people receive, narrative conversations can be political actions in which the intent is to decolonise identity stories. (Drahm-Butler, 2015, p. 29)

[See DECOLONISATION; DECOLONISATION IS NOT A METAPHOR]

Deconstruction Originated by the philosopher Jacques Derrida (2016) as an approach to unpack the assumptions upon which any text is based. Certain aspects of narrative practice can be framed as deconstruction or as a deconstructive method:

> According to my rather loose definition, deconstruction has to do with procedures that subvert taken-for-granted realities and practices; those so-called 'truths' that are split off from the conditions and the context of their production, those disembodied ways of speaking that hide their biases and prejudices, and those familiar practices of self and of relationship that are subjugating of persons' lives. Many of the methods of deconstruction render strange these familiar and everyday taken-for-granted realities and practices by objectifying them … we can also consider deconstruction in other senses: for example, the deconstruction of self-narrative and the dominant cultural knowledges that persons live by; the deconstruction of practices of self and of relationship that are dominantly cultural; and the deconstruction of the discursive practices of our culture. (White, 1991, p. 27)

> Narrative therapists help clients deconstruct the dominant social and cultural messages that serve to oppress them. Narrative therapy is thus situated between the political and the personal. Because individual problems are assumed to be rooted in an oppressive social system, rather than in the individual, as is the case within traditional psychoanalysis, individual change is linked to political change in the narrative therapy approach. The narrative therapy approach may be particularly well suited for women and other members of oppressed groups because it does not focus on adjustment, like traditional therapies, but analyzes and questions social and cultural narratives of domination. This questioning of domination is consistent with feminist aims. Thus, narrative therapy can be seen as a feminist practice of self insofar as it aims at self-transformation and aims towards a particular goal, resisting the dominant discourse. (McLaren, 2002, p. 162)

[See BINARY THINKING; CONSCIOUSNESS-RAISING; DISCOURSE]

Definitional ceremony

> Socially marginalized people. Disdained, ignored groups. Individuals with what Erving Goffman calls 'spoiled identities', regularly seek opportunities to appear before others in the light of the own internally provided interpretation … I have called such performances 'Definitional ceremonies', understanding them to be collective self-definitions specifically intended to proclaim an interpretation to an audience not otherwise available. (Myerhoff, 1982, p. 105)

Barbara Myerhoff's concept of definitional ceremony is explicitly 'political'. Marc Kaminsky describes this in more detail:

> Myerhoff worked up the concept of 'definitional ceremonies' in two important case studies of the discursive forms used by 'oppressed people' to wage political fights … Myerhoff includes storytelling, public rituals, and ceremonies, meetings, murals, protest marches, and other enactments and displays under this category. The genre-shaping intention that these have in common is the intention to affirm the individual by grounding her personal identity and worth in the culture and social history of the group. In practice, this assertion of value is polemical and oppositional: it is made against the dominant social evaluation which denies the meaning and value of the group's culture and social history. Hence, the intention is to contest the evaluative and interpretive social discourse of the dominant culture (ageism, sexism, anti-Semitism, devaluation of working-class and poor people). (Kaminsky, 1992, pp. 17–18 in footnote no. 5).

Definitional ceremony structures have been used within therapeutic contexts:

> The definitional ceremony metaphor structures the therapeutic arena as a context for the rich description of people's lives, identities and relationships. This metaphor structures rituals that are acknowledging of and 'regrading' of people's lives, in contrast to many of the common rituals of modern culture that are judging of and 'degrading' of lives. I have drawn the definitional ceremony metaphor from the work of Barbara Myerhoff (1982, 1986), a cultural anthropologist, and have developed therapeutic applications of this metaphor. (White, 2003, p. 54)

Definitional ceremony *(continued)*

Definitional ceremony structures have also been used within community projects and collective narrative practice:

> These ceremonies described by Myerhoff (1986) were forms of social action … collective narrative practice seeks to bring together considerations of meaning-making, identity-formation, enabling contribution and social action. It seems relevant to mention here that definitional ceremonies, as described by Myerhoff, have a great deal to offer us in this endeavour.
>
> Her descriptions invite us to remember that 'identity formation' and 'social action' are not separate. Convening definitional ceremonies around, and in relation to, various initiatives of social action that people are taking can powerfully influence not only these people's self-definition, but also their ability to continue to take action.
>
> Finding ways to convene ceremonies in which people act as outsider witnesses and as engaged participants joined in social projects for a broader good, is one of the aims of collective narrative practice. (Denborough, 2008, pp. 65–66)

Democratising the field of narrative practice

Folk cultural methodologies such as the Tree of Life and Team of Life were deliberately developed so that narrative therapy and community work ideas can be engaged with, not only by highly trained professionals, but also by key community and family leaders who may not have had the privilege of extensive schooling or education. This is what David Denborough refers to as 'democratising narrative practice':

> How can we ensure that narrative ways of working can be put into practice by aunties, uncles, mothers, fathers and community leaders, especially in contexts where highly trained professionals may be few and far between? (Denborough, 2018, p. 54).

[See TREE OF LIFE; TEAM OF LIFE]

Diagnostic Statistical Manual of Mental Disorders (DSM)

The Diagnostic Statistical Manual was originally a discourse about medical symptoms for researchers. However the DSM escaped the laboratory and found its way into public, administrative and professional discourses. For the narrative therapist understanding the DSM's medical focus on individual symptomatology as well as how decontextualized prescriptions for practice get named becomes critical to their understandings in conversational work. The DSM's push to locate problems inside client bodies and defining these problems as individual deficits or symptoms to be treated individually, obscures vital information. Danish research psychologist, Svend Brinkmann (2016) writes of 'diagnostic cultures' where DSM diagnoses, like ADHD or depression, are becoming central to one's identity. In other words, diagnosis-related stories become interwoven with everyday life, often in ways that foretell of, or perhaps foreclose on life possibilities. (Madigan, 2019, p. 191)

Dignity

Story can break the dignity of a people but story can also repair that broken dignity. (Adichie, 2009)

Disability

This entry was written by Tiffany Sostar and Gipsy Hosking

Dominant discourses of disability often locate the problem within the individual and the solution as one of building resilience and strength of character. However, disability justice advocates locate the problem in the disabling physical and social environments that surround a person. Further, disability advocates draw a distinction between 'impairment' as the physical or mental differences in the body and 'disability' as produced by the environment. These discourses are socially constructed, and can be deconstructed and reauthored. In this approach 'disability' is understood as an effect of power relations sustained through the systematic privileging of the abled-bodied. As Rosmarie Garland-Thomson explains (2006), the able-bodied/disability hierarchical binary is used to 'legitimate an unequal distribution of resources, status and power within a biased social and architectural environment' (p. 259).

Disability *(continued)*

There have recently been significant shifts in discourses of disability, and this is a rich area of work and theorizing. The concept of 'nothing about us without us', which has been taken up in so much narrative practice, has roots in 1990s disability activism in South Africa, Eastern Europe, and North America. This challenging of existing hierarchies of knowledge brings disability justice work and narrative practice into alignment, both locating people as experts in their own experiences, both valuing insider knowledges, and both exploring the social construction of identities. As an example of shifting discourses, autistic advocates have pushed to understand autism as neurodiversity rather than disability. Sparrow Rose Jones writes,

> [M]y mind is unstrange: I am not a different species, an alien creature, a changeling, a robot, a freak of nature. I am a familiar word, pronounced with a different accent … I am a human being; I am Autistic. (Jones, 2013, p. 3)

Narrative therapy has engaged with 'relocating the problem of disability' (Kunc, Van der Klift, Reynolds, Munro, 2015), and with questioning the underlying cultural stories that shape disability discourses.

> People with disabilities are not oppressed by what we can or cannot do with our bodies or minds. We may be inconvenienced by living with an impairment, but what oppresses us is the systemic prejudice, discrimination, segregation and violence we face because we do not fall within a perceived 'norm'. (Berne, Milbern & Weiner-Mahfuz, n.d.)

Recent research by the First Peoples Disability Network (Avery, 2018), offers an Aboriginal and Torres Strait Islander perspective on disability:

> The small amount of published research on disability in Aboriginal and Torres Strait Islander communities all settle on a conclusion that 'disability' is not a concept that readily translates in Aboriginal languages and cultures … The contemporary dilemma for Aboriginal and Torres Strait Islander people is that their culture and belief system of human functioning and diversity is so radically different from the Western construct of disability dominant in Australia and other Westernised nations. The Western system constructs disability as a deficit against a perceived 'normal level of functioning', and

> 'an individual deficit/problem that has to be fixed, rehabilitated or prevented' (Berghs et.al, 2016). Philosophical reflections aside, the cultural dichotomies present a contemporary dilemma for Aboriginal and Torres Strait Islander people. 'Do you have a disability?' is a question that is culturally insensible for Indigenous peoples. (Avery, 2018, pp. 4–5)

Other disability justice practitioners point to the cultural work involved in figuring out how to live in an ableist world:

> The transition itself, of becoming disabled or moving along the ability spectrum, is frequently invisibilized, to the point that these changes do not even have a name. We do not have a way to talk about becoming disabled or more impaired. I feel like society not having language to describe this transition or the support it requires speaks to the ableism and isolation people with disability face in our lives. Of course there aren't yet words for this. Without crip intervention, we are frequently left alone to figure out how to be in our bodyminds in this ableist world. (Stacey Milbern quoted in Piepzna-Samarasinha, 2018, p. 240)

Beyond the individual and the social models of disability is a third embodied approach that recognises that we experience the world through the particular body that we are in and attempts to bring the body back into the social or discursive model of disability. This embodied approach points out that focusing exclusively on discriminatory discourses and social barriers 'render pain and fatigue [and other bodily symptoms and sensations] irrelevant to the project of disability politics'. (Kafer, 2013, p. 7)

To view philosophies which some young people with disabilities use to endure ableism and other challenges, see: https://dulwichcentre.com.au/philosophies

[See ABLEISM]

Discourse

The concept of discourse used in narrative therapy derives from Michel Foucault (2012) who claimed to have used the term in about seventeen different ways. He argued that in the modern world, power relations are formed around the control of discourse rather than just around the fear of physical threat.

Discourses shape …

> … our thoughts, ideas, beliefs, values, identities, interactions with others, and our behaviour … Sociologists see discourse as embedded in and emerging out of relations of power … as such, discourse, power, and knowledge are intimately connected, and work together to create hierarchies. Some discourses come to dominate the mainstream (dominant discourses), and are considered truthful, normal, and right, while others are marginalized and stigmatized, and considered wrong, extreme, and even dangerous … the power of discourse lies in its ability to provide legitimacy for certain kinds of knowledge while undermining others; and, in its ability to create subject positions, and, to turn people into objects that can be controlled. (Cole, 2018)

[See SMASH THAT DISCOURSE; DECONSTRUCTION]

Disembodied speech (and questions that insist on embodiment)

[Disembodied] … 'expert' ways of speaking include those that (a) obscure the motives or purposes that are associated with one's speech acts, (b) delete all reference to the personal experiences through which one's knowledge claims are generated, (c) exclude information about the personal and interpersonal struggles and dilemmas that are associated with the construction of one's preferred realities (this includes the erasure of the personal experiences of contestation and argumentation through which one's knowledge claims are established), (d) divert attention from the personal investments that are informed by one's location in the social worlds of gender, race, culture, class, work, sexual preference, and so on, and (e) delete all reference to the history of controversy and dissent that surrounds all 'global' knowledge claims.

… the persuasiveness and impressiveness of such [disembodied] speech acts can be undermined by the principle of embodiment; that is, by situating these speech acts within the context of the speaker's (a) motives and purposes, (b) personal experiences, including those that relate to dilemmas and other struggles that the speaker has experienced in the process of attributing meaning to their experiences of life, (c) investments that are informed by their location in the social worlds of gender, culture, race, class, sexual preference, and so on, and also by bringing forth the history of controversy that surrounds the speaker's objective knowledge claims …

To encourage speakers to situate their opinions in the context of their purposes, we could ask questions like: *So you have a strong opinion about what I should do. Tell me, in voicing your opinion in this way, what effect do you hope this might have on what I do?* Or maybe we could ask: *If you were to succeed in influencing what I do on this occasion, how would this fit with your overall goals for my life?* Or perhaps: *I think that I have some understanding of how you*

Disembodied speech (and questions that insist on embodiment)
(continued)

would like your opinion to shape what I do right now. How does this fit with your general purposes for my life? How does this fit with your plans for my life?

To encourage speakers to situate their opinions in the context of their lived experience, we could try something like: *Could you tell me about some of your personal experiences of life that have played a central role in the formation of this opinion? This would be helpful to me, as I would then know more about how to take your opinion, and I might be able to identify those parts of your views that could fit for me. Perhaps I could then talk of some of my own experiences of life, and share with you some of the conclusions that I have reached from all of this.*

To encourage speakers to situate their opinions within the context of their location in the social world, we might try something like: *In which circles are these sort of opinions most strongly held? Do all of the people in these circles agree with this opinion? If some of these people were here with us, how would they go about supporting your opinion? What do you think would happen if, in their presence, you were to dissent? What sort of pressure do you think you would experience to conform, to recant? What consequences do you think you would be facing if you didn't agree to do so?*

But this is just a small sample of the possibilities for ways of responding that are deconstructing of the 'truths' that are championed in disembodied speech acts. And I want to emphasise that these questions do not require an answer in order to be effective. In asking such questions, those who are subject to disembodied speech acts become less captive, and are confronted with new possibilities for action. (White, 1995b, pp. 128–130)

Documents of identity

In times of stress – when we find ourselves under significant duress when facing situations of adversity – we are all vulnerable to being separated from our knowledgeableness. At these times, we often experience a dearth of creative responses to the situations we find ourselves in; our usual problem-solving skills don't seem available to us, and our options for action seem to evaporate. Our focus of attention can become very narrow, we can begin to lose our sense of identity and, at times, when the stress that we are subject to is particularly acute, we can undergo something akin to paralysis.

Now, those people who have experienced psychotic episodes are ever so much more vulnerable to being dispossessed of their knowledgeableness and their preferred sense of identity at such times. And it is this dispossession that sets the scene for the experience of great personal insecurity and distress, and for further acute episodes. So it makes a great deal of sense for these people to carry with them, at all times, documents of their identity. These are documents that they can consult under those circumstances when they are losing sight of their knowledgeableness, when their sense of identity is at risk …

There are many aspects to these documents, and many possible forms. Such documents can include some historical account of the person's ability to intervene, on his or her own behalf, in his/her own life. This is an account of personal agency, an account that emphasises, what could be called the person's 'agentive self'. It includes details about what the person has been up against in the performance of this personal agency, and, against this background, emphasises the significance of any more recent steps that the person has been taking toward having more to say about how their life goes.

These documents are grounded in hope; for example, they often include details about the sort of personal qualities and other characteristics that were available to the person in the earlier years of their life, and speculation about how, when, and under what circumstances these might resurface in the service of the person's own plans and goals. These documents can also include details about any recent developments in the person's problem-solving skills.

Documents of identity *(continued)*

Because other people's responses to the sort of identity claims that are reflected in these documents are of critical importance, those people who might provide an appropriate audience to this alternative account of the person's identity are specifically referred to in these documents. This is achieved in a way that is less likely to leave the response of this audience to chance – the wording is put in such a way as to invite acknowledging responses from this audience.

… It is not uncommon for the people who consult me to carry several documents of this sort on their person at all times. This way, they are ever available to be consulted. This considerably alleviates people's anxiety in the face of the trials and tribulations of everyday existence, and renders them less vulnerable to acute episodes. (White, 1995b, pp. 142–145)

[See ALTERNATIVE TEXTS]

Dominant story (sometimes referred to as the problem story)

A narrative can never re-present the richness of what Turner (1986) has called our 'lived experience': … *life experience is richer than discourse. Narrative structures organize and give meaning to experience, but there are always feelings and lived experience not fully encompassed by the dominant story.* (Bruner 1986, p. 143) (White, 1988a, p. 23)

In all of our lives, there will be events that make us cringe, those that bring heartache, those that bring sorrow, those that bring shame. If those moments are all linked together into a storyline, we can feel truly hopeless about life. But in all of our lives, there will also be events or small moments of beauty, or kindness, or respite, or escape, or defiance. When these events are linked together to tell a story about us, then life becomes easier to live. (Denborough, 2014, p. 7)

[See COUNTERSTORIES]

Double comfort

> The acknowledgment of privilege seems to strike a chord for racially-aware members of the dominant group, but I would propose that admitting one's privilege does not necessarily unsettle its operation. For this is a concept that has the potential to leave those who name it in a place of double comfort: the comfort of demonstrating that one is critically aware, and the comfort of not needing to act to undo privilege. (Heron, 2005, p. 344)

Double consciousness

> W.E.B. Du Bois (1903) described the phenomenon of *double consciousness* in which all too commonly the colonized begins to judge their own behaviour, actions, looks, relationships by the standards of the colonizers. (Akinyela, 2002, p. 36)

Double listening (or Doubly listening)

A term Michael White used to refer to a posture of listening for hardship *and* people's *responses* to hardship; listening for any expression of distress *and also* to what is absent but implicit in this expression of distress (in other words, what treasured value has been violated in order to bring about this experience of distress).

> The engagement with this interest in the absent but implicit requires, and is reinforcing of, a double listening on behalf of the therapist. It is in the context of this double listening that people experience being doubly or multiply heard. This is a context in which people find that there is space for them to express their experience of whatever it is that troubles them. And, as well, it is in this context that they have the opportunity to explore the unstated; that is, whatever it is that this discernment speaks to. In this way, the engagement with this interest in the absent but implicit contributes to therapeutic conversations as double- or multi-storied conversations. (White, 2000a, p. 41)

[See ABSENT BUT IMPLICIT]

Double-storied testimonies

David Denborough has described a framework for eliciting and documenting 'double-storied testimonies':

> Part of this work involves interviewing and documenting the stories of individuals and communities who have experienced significant trauma. Significantly, we do more than only document the experience of trauma. We also document the ways in which these individuals and communities have responded to this trauma, their initiatives, their acts and skills of resistance and healing, their hopes and values, and the histories of these hopes and values. As a result, the testimonies that are created can be understood to be 'double-storied testimonies'.
>
> … It's my hope that this framework will assist others to receive and document testimonies in ways that are not re-traumatising and that, in fact, contribute to redressing the effects of trauma in the person's life. The documents that are created can then be used for broader purposes including:
>
> - to share with others who have been through similar experiences;
> - to educate professionals about the skills and knowledge of those who have survived traumatic experiences;
> - to raise community awareness about the effects of trauma and violence in order to play a part in reducing the likelihood of further abuses;
> - to facilitate broader political/community action;
> - to seek forms of individual or social acknowledgement;
> - to seek formal redress/justice. (Denborough, 2006, pp. 116–117)

e

Emotion

Narrative therapy engages with emotion in a particular way. It couples emotion and meaning, and refuses to separate them. It also refuses to separate emotion and meaning from action. In this way, emotion is also never separated from culture, politics and ethics. Here are two quotes from Michael White about this:

> It's really to do with . . . not thinking about the role of emotions but thinking of how all expressions are expressions of experience, units of feeling, units of meaning, units of action, not divided up into one or the other. So there's a refusal to get into this dualism around feeling versus meanings, or feelings versus action. (M. White, 2002b)

> I've always avoided talking about feelings in the literature because it gets taken up into that time honoured dualism . . . if someone is expressing powerful emotion I'm interested in that expression but I'm also interested in where that expression is taking them to that they might not have otherwise gotten to, if they hadn't been expressing that. And I think that's a lot more honouring of what we call 'emotional expression' because it's not just discharging something, it's also an action that's taking someone to a certain place. There's also a meaning and a sentiment expressed in it. You know, that person is opening their life to me, and taking a step in their relationship with me as well. (M. White, 2002b)

Significantly, narrative practice is also interested in the real effects of how 'emotions' are understood and practiced in particular times, places and cultures. For more about how narrative practice engages with emotion see Denborough (in press).

Enabling contribution

Many of the people with whom we work have very little chance to feel as if they are making a contribution to the lives of others. They may feel hopeless, that they can't even get their own life together, let alone offer something to someone else. The difficulties that people are facing, however, will not be theirs alone, and their experience of hardship and how they have responded to hardship *can* offer a contribution to others in similar or related situations. Significantly, the experience of making a contribution to the lives of others can be the catalyst to reduce the effects (or transform the nature) of the suffering in the person's life. When the hardwon knowledge they have gained through adversity contributes to someone else who is in the midst of similar struggle, this can bring a sense that their suffering has 'not been for nothing' (Myerhoff, 1982, p. 111). This can spark a sense of possibility that can ripple over to other aspects of their life.

In our experience, the more difficult the circumstances a community is facing, the more significant this principle becomes. So much so, that over recent years this principle has led us to reconfigure our work. People enduring significant hardship are often seen to be requiring 'help', 'healing', 'therapy', or 'psychosocial support' and it is often assumed that this 'help' is to be provided through professional services. But perhaps something quite different is required. Perhaps what is required is for contexts to be created in which individuals and communities who are going through hard times can make contributions to the lives of others who are going through similar difficulties. (Denborough, 2008, pp. 3–4)

Environmental action

[See PLACE; PLACE AND ENVIRONMENTAL ACTION]

Escaping normality

With the advent of the pervasiveness of modern power, finding ways to escape normality and normalising judgment becomes more significant.

> In order to revise the storylines of our lives, we may need to question 'normality' and find escape routes from experiences of failure. (Denborough, 2014, p. 147)

[See MODERN POWER]

Essentialism

> … the belief that 'human nature', an individual's personality, or some specific quality … is an innate and natural 'essence' (rather than a product of circumstances, upbringing, and culture). (Chandler & Munday, 2016)

> … humanist essentialism … asserts the existence of certain elements and substances that make up a self that is at the centre of who we are … that takes for granted not only the existence of this self, but that there is a 'truth' of human nature to be found in these essences, and that this represents what is 'original' about being human. (White, 2000b, p. 106)

[See NON-ESSENTIALIST UNDERSTANDINGS; POSTSTRUCTURALISM]

Establishing political appreciation of a person's experience of abuse

In the following extract, from an interview by Chris McLean (White, 1995c), Michael White speaks of the importance of establishing an appreciation of the politics of a person's experience of abuse:

Chris: I'd like now to explore your views on the importance of establishing a political or contextual appreciation of a person's experience of abuse, and in particular, how the concept of recruitment fits into this idea.

Michael: To assist people to establish an account of the politics of their experience helps to undermine the self-blame and the shame that is so often experienced in relation to the abuse itself. One way that this can be achieved is through engaging with people in externalizing conversations about the self-hate, self-loathing, or whatever it is that constitutes the person's primary relationship with their 'self'. In these externalizing conversations, we can explore with people what this self-hate talks them into about who they are as people, how it has them treating their lives, their bodies, their thoughts, how it interferes in their relationships with others, and so on. And together we can also explore the processes by which the person was recruited into self-hate and self-loathing.

Chris: So you emphasise questions about how the person got recruited into self-hate, or self-loathing, or whatever, and this has the effect of bringing forth the politics of the person's experience?

Michael: Yes, it is primarily through such questions that this is achieved. It is through such questions that we wind up identifying the specifics of this process of recruitment – not just the physical processes of abuse, but also the knowledges, the strategies and the techniques that were employed, and the workings of these knowledges, strategies and techniques. But we would not arrive at this place by referencing our work to the idea of returning to the site of the trauma. In responding to these externalizing questions people are actually engaging in a reinterpretation of their experiences of abuse, and are breaking from the negative stories of identity that have been so capturing of them.

Establishing political appreciation of a person's experience of abuse

(continued)

> No longer can the abuse reflect personal culpability, and no longer does it reflect to people the truth of their 'nature' and of their 'personality'. I believe that these externalizing conversations can be considered as 'deconstructing' conversations.
>
> Perhaps another way of stating this, one that is inspired by the narrative metaphor, is that the reinterpretation that is triggered by these questions provides a basis for a renaming of the dominant plots of people's lives – away from themes of personal culpability, and towards exploitation, tyranny, abuse, and so on. (White, 1995c, pp. 88–89)

Ethic of collaboration

In contrast to an ethic of control:

> … an ethic of collaboration … brings with it a different account of effective action. Effective action is recast. Rather than singular and independent action that is delivered into persons' lives, the ethic of collaboration recasts effective action as that which is determined and taken in partnership with others. And, rather than action that is measured by its success in the achievement of sought-after ends in a time-frame that is specified ahead of the initiation of this action, the ethic of collaboration recasts effective action as those actions that consist of the steps that contribute to the establishment of a foundation of possibility in persons' lives in the time that is required to take these steps. (White, 1997, p. 198)

In conceptualising an ethic of collaboration, Michael White drew significantly on feminist writer Sharon Welch's *A Feminist Ethic of Risk* (1990).

[See ETHIC OF CONTROL]

Ethic of control

> Linked to a notion of effective action that implies therapists (and others) ought 'to achieve sought-after ends in a specified and usually brief period of time through singular and independent action … rarely are the contexts of therapy ones that are at all favourable or amenable to accounts of effective action that are informed by this ethic of control'. (White, 1997, p. 197).

[See ETHIC OF COLLABORATION]

Examining silences

One of the dimensions of critical thinking described by Mary Heath (2012):

> We can also ask who is speaking about this claim or proposal, and what are they saying. If more than one voice is present, what do you notice about the differences in what each voice contributes? Who is silent? Why are they silent? Who is silenced – not allowed to speak, not reported as speaking, not listened to if they do speak? It is helpful to consider our own silences: are they chosen by ourselves or encouraged by others? Does speaking involve penalties? Are there places where we speak? In what ways do our decisions to speak prevent others from speaking? How could we enable their speech? Is it possible that the way we speak creates silences? (p. 16)

Exoticising the domestic

This notion of 'exoticising the domestic' (Bourdieu 1988, pp. xi-xii) has been of assistance to me in my efforts to characterise explorations of narrative practice. This seems entirely resonant with a form of therapeutic inquiry in which investigations of 'the ordinary world' culminate in investigations of 'alien and extraordinary worlds' … Amongst other things … [narrative practices] … exoticise modern notions about the nature of life and identity that are considered to be universally true, generally relevant, and globally applicable. They also exoticise unquestioned cultural practices that are instrumental in inciting people to bring their lives into harmony with the socially constructed norms of contemporary western culture. And, furthermore … [narrative practices] exoticise some of the taken-for-granted counselling conventions that have the potential to reproduce the very contexts that are generative of the problems and predicaments that people bring to therapy.

So much about modern rationality obscures, diminishes and marginalises diversity in modes of life and thought. As a consequence of this, people's lives are rendered routine and, in a great many circumstances, sub-ordinary. The sentiment associated with 'exoticising the domestic' can provide an antidote to these effects of this modern rationality by encouraging therapeutic inquiry into what is unique in people's lives. In the context of inquiry shaped by this sentiment, the territories of people's lives that are routinely considered lacklustre and monotonous are rendered exotic. And in the context of inquiry shaped by this sentiment, therapeutic conversations that might otherwise reproduce the known and the familiar, become journeys to destinations that cannot be specified or predicted in advance of arrival.

'I hope that you will join me in working to ...
cultivate the resurrection of diversity in everyday life.'

Michael White

Exoticising the domestic *(continued)*

> This sentiment associated with 'exoticising the domestic' sponsors a form of therapeutic inquiry in which people suddenly find themselves interested in novel understandings of the events of their lives, curious about aspects of their lives that have been forsaken, fascinated with neglected territories of their identities, and, at times, awed by their own responses to the predicaments of their existence. For therapists, this sentiment fosters a consciousness of the lifeshaping aspects of therapeutic inquiry, including a consciousness of the ways in which we, as therapists, are becoming other than who we were at the outset of our meetings with the people who consult us. This consciousness contributes significantly to the rich story development of our own lives and work, and can be a source of inspiration ... I hope that you will join me in working to further develop therapeutic practices that have the potential to 'exoticise the domestic', that will contribute to the identification of 'extraordinary worlds', and that will cultivate the resurrection of diversity in everyday life. (White, 2004a, vi-vii)

Exposé

One of the key purposes of externalising conversations is to enable an exposé of the operations of problems:

> We cannot here emphasise strongly enough how important it is to have the opportunity to speak of the troublesome voices and visions in a forum that contributes to a powerful exposé of their purposes and their operations. (Brigitte, Sue, Mem & Veronika, 1997, p. 205)

[See EXTERNALISING]

Exposing oppressive social forces

Externalising conversations have now been applied to a wide range of purposes, including to assist people to situate their problems in the political, cultural, and socio/economic contexts of their lives. (White, 2002a, p. 152) For example, Brian Williams and Barbara Baumgartner (2014) asked the following questions with the intention of exposing various oppressive social forces:

- How did racism / sexism / transphobia / homophobia / ableism make using crack cocaine an easier option for you to take up?
- Did growing up in a working family that struggled to make ends meet make anxiety stronger or weaker for you? How did it do that?
- What is the relationship between homelessness and crystal meth use? How did your use of meth make homelessness more manageable? Was there a turning point when meth started to fuel homelessness more than it was fuelling you?
- How did social stigma about your schizophrenia diagnosis affect the job options that were available to you?
- Who knows about your ability to resist the influence of depression? What might they tell me they know about you that leads them to believe you can overcome it?
- Who stands with you now against psychosis, and how might we invite them to get more involved in supporting you? (Williams and Baumgartner, 2014, p. 249)

[See EXTERNALISING]

Externalising

'… Externalising is a principle or a philosophy that refuses to locate problems inside people … This way of thinking refuses to pathologize people. Instead, we can acknowledge that problems have histories. They are created over time. And often problems are affected by broader factors, like poverty, racism, and sexism. This is not to diminish the seriousness of the problem or its effects. Many people struggle with the effects of overwhelming hardship. This makes it all the more important that we speak about these problems and understand them in ways that are separate from the person. The person is not the problem; the problem is the problem ...' (Denborough, 2014, p. 27)

- How long has *The Anxiety* (or *The Depression* or *The Self-Hate* or *The Voice of Abuse*) been a resident in your life?
- When did __________ first come into your life?
- When is it most likely to visit? Does it come announced or unannounced?
- What are the 'friends' of this problem? Does it work in tandem with other factors (like poverty, gender injustice, or racism)?
- What are the times and places where it is most powerful?

(Denborough, 2014, pp. 34–35)

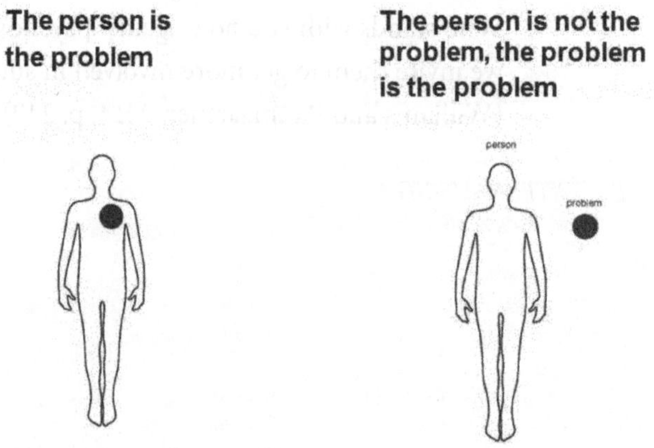

Figure 1. Externalizing problems.

'... externalizing conversations emphasise the politics of experience.'

Michael White

Externalising

(continued)

... internalizing conversations obscure the politics of experience, externalizing conversations emphasise the politics of experience. And whenever the politics of experience is emphasised, there are possibilities for deconstruction. (White, 1995d, p. 24)

While practices associated with the externalizing of problems enable persons to separate themselves and their relationships from such problems, these practices do not separate persons from responsibility for the extent to which they participate in the survival of the problem. In fact, as these practices help persons become aware of and describe their relationship with the problem, they enable them to assume responsibility for the problem, something they could not do beforehand. The practices associated with the externalizing of problems also (a) free persons from problem-saturated descriptions of their lives and relationships, (b) encourage the generation or resurrection of alternative and more rewarding stories of lives and relationships, and (c) assist persons to identify and develop a new relationship with the problem. In so doing, these practices foster a new sense of personal agency; with this, persons are able to assume responsibility for the investigation of new choices in their lives and to pursue new possibilities. In the process, they experience a newfound capacity to intervene in their world. (White & Epston, 1990, p. 65)

[See THE PERSON IS NOT THE PROBLEM, THE PROBLEM IS THE PROBLEM; EXPOSING OPPRESSIVE SOCIAL FORCES]

f

Failure

> The phenomenon of personal failure has grown exponentially over recent decades. Never before has the sense of being a failure to be an adequate person been so freely available to people, and never before has it been so willingly and routinely dispensed. (White, 2002a, p. 151)

Narrative practice can involve questioning 'normality' and thereby transforming the meaning of experiences of failure (see Hutton, 2008).

[See ESCAPING NORMALITY; MODERN POWER]

Family therapy

> Many people nowadays don't know how radical the notion of family therapy was. Michael White, as you know, was a family therapist and one of the founding members and inaugural editor of the Australian Journal of Family Therapy (which went on to become the Australia and New Zealand Journal of Family Therapy). In the early 1980s, family therapy was still trying to carve out a new field based on the idea of seeing more than one person of the family in the session. In psychotherapy, prior to family therapy, the family was overwhelmingly seen as toxic: you needn't speak to the family, because the family was seen as the cause of the person's problem. Working with the family in the session was therefore seen as unsound. Unfortunately, the remnants of these ideas continue to be influential today, and it remains most common for psychotherapists to see individuals only, rather than include family members, friends, and partners in the therapy room. The idea of working with everybody in a family was a radical notion. (Findlay, 2016, p. 19)

Feminism

Feminism is a politics. It is a politics directed at changing existing power relations between women and men in society. (Weedon, 1987, p. 1)

… feminist theory and political practice have as a goal the critique and transformation of a set of relations of power – a set defined by the intersection of sexism, racism, class oppression, and heterosexism, to name only a few of the most conspicuous axes. (Allen, 1996, p. 266)

Chrystos (2003), writing from a First Nations two-spirit perspective:

When I got involved with feminism, I was involved with the battered women's shelter movement and that movement was started by women who were formerly battered. It was very much a grass roots organization, very powerful. It was a turning point in my life. It was the turning point in many women's lives. And now, in order to work in a battered women's shelter, you have to have a Masters Degree. It's like there's this whole way in which the academic world and the government have taken over the battered women's shelter movement so it has now become professional white collar … and as far as I can tell there's no feminist agenda that talks about Native rights. I've been hollering my head off for thirty years. I still run into anger from women who feel like I'm personally and directly insulting them by what I talk about. That's actually from class privilege. (Chrystos, 2003, p. 14)

Feminisms, intersectionality and narrative practice

A project initiated by Cheryl White, see: www.dulwichcentre.com.au/feminisms, involving narrative practitioners from many different social locations.

Feminist challenge to therapists

Over years, some feminist thinkers have explicitly challenged therapists … Perhaps the most well-known of these recent challenges appears in the book *'Changing our Minds'* by Celia Kitzinger and Rachel Perkins (1993). Kitzinger and Perkins, writing specifically as lesbian feminists about the application of therapy to lesbian lives, argue that therapy is inherently a process of psychologising and individualising women's experience when these are clearly issues of political inequity. Therapeutic practices, they believe, replicate the oppression of women by constructing their distress as individual 'maladjustments' rather than as a result of constantly attempting to adjust to society's patriarchal expectations. Kitzinger and Perkins' book is one we would recommend to all feminist therapists as it challenges us to develop ways of working with the stories of women's lives that do not individualise what are broader social relations, that do not psychologise experience, and that do not reduce politics to healing. (Russell & Carey, 2003, p. 80)

Feminist dictionary

A word book which calls into question the androcentric nature of much 'standard language usage' and problematizes many words and phrases in the light of feminist perspectives and commentary. *This* feminist dictionary (1) recognizes women as linguistically creative speakers, (2) explicitly acknowledges the socio-political aspects of dictionary-making, (3) draws heavily on excerpted material from feminist publications, (4) does not generally specify 'parts of speech' (noun, verb, etc.) or linguistic status (coinage, obsolete, etc.) but rather provides commentary on the general cultural knowledge that the readers bring to this book, (5) assumes that a book about words is inevitably a book about the world as well, (6) emphasizes definitions by feminists without making continual reference to male authorities, (7) sometimes offers 'contradictions' without resolving them. That this book is incomplete goes without saying. (Kramarae & Treichler, 1985, pp. 161–162)

Feminist family therapists

> Early feminist family therapists began to bring an analysis of gender into therapeutic inquiry. These women included Rachel Hare-Mustin (1978, 1987, Hare-Mustin & Marecek 1990), Marianne Walters, Betty Carter, Peggy Papp and Olga Silverstein of the Women's Project in New York (1988), and Monica McGoldrick, Carol Anderson and Froma Walsh (1989). Here in Australia, Kerrie James' influential keynote address, 'Breaking the chains of gender' was an early example (see James 2001; James & McIntyre 1983). These feminist inquiries opened up new ways of understanding people's lives and family relationships and therefore created new possibilities as to ways of talking about the problems people brought to therapy. (Russell & Carey, 2003, p. 71)

Feminist influence on narrative therapy

Cheryl White (2016) describes:

> The 1970s and 1980s were a time of profound feminist challenge in the therapy field. Ann Epston and I, Michael [White], and David [Epston] were all vitally engaged with and influenced by the feminist issues of that time. Everything was up for questioning: the gender roles in families, the practices of mother-blaming, the concept of 'schizophrenogenic mothers', gender inequities in the field of family therapy, male-centred language, heterosexual dominance, the politics of representation, and so on … For me, the early 1970s was a time of enormous recognition of other women. And there is no doubt that Women's Liberation and feminist politicising of everyday life was a significant influence in Australian family therapy in the 1980s and one of the key threads in the development of narrative practice. (White, 2016, pp. 48–50)

Feminist practice of the self

[See CONSCIOUNESS-RAISING; DECONSTRUCTION]

Full memories

In order to re-associate dissociated memories, it is necessary to restore these half memories to full memories. In other words, the task is to resurrect that which is erased in dissociated memory – that is, people's responses to what they were being put through, and the foundations of these responses. This resurrection is restorative of a sense of personal agency, one that is in harmony with the person's preferred 'sense of myself'. This is the 'sense of myself' … one that provides an experience of continuity of personhood through the many episodes of one's history. The restoration of these memories to full memories provides the foundation for them to be taken into history in the storylines of people's lives – in being restored in these ways, these memories carry with them accounts of personhood that are no longer alien, and this provides conditions for these memories to be taken into the storylines of people's lives in ways that provides them with beginnings and endings in time. When traumatic memory is re-associated in this way, the potential for these memories to be re-traumatising is very significantly diminished. (White, 2004b, pp. 79–80).

[See HALF MEMORIES]

g

Gender and culture together

Taimalieutu Kiwi Tamasese describes:

> As women from subjugated cultures we have tried to point out that gender and culture cannot be separated. Our ways of living … are always influenced by the symbols, rituals, language and relationship structures of culture. Recognising that gender cannot be separated from culture does not mean that we are privileging culture over gender. It means that whenever we are talking about gender, cultural considerations are relevant, as are other considerations of class and sexuality etc. Similarly, wherever we are talking about culture, relations of gender are relevant. (Tamasese, 2007, p. 100)

[See LIBERATIVE GENDER ARRANGEMENTS]

Gender dichotomy

Gender dichotomy refers to the concept that only two distinct sexes and/or genders exist, with no other scientifically or culturally accepted alternatives outside the realms of pathology. The dichotomy is strongly … supported by … expressions like: 'the opposite sex', 'the opposite gender', 'gender crossing', 'cross dressing', and so on. In gender related scientific literature, the dichotomy appears in … conceptions like: 'to label oneself boy or girl', 'man or woman', 'to be confused or uncertain whether one is boy or girl', 'the basic sense of self as either a male or female', and many, many others. (Benestad, 2016, p. 97)

Gender fluid

Gender fluid refers to people who do not prescribe to any particular gender expression, who will 'play around' with multiple gendered expressions. (Benestad, 2016, p. 97)

Gender identity

Gender identity refers to a person's basic sense of self as woman or man, or both as woman and man, some third category, or gender dismissal. (Benestad, 2016, p. 97)

Gendered personification of problems

It's interesting how often in the narrative practice of personifying the problem, that the problem gets gendered as a male, from Mr Mischief to Tommy Trouble. I wonder about the gendered assumptions that we may be making in relation to the nature of problems and the effect that this might have on people's relationships with those problems. I am interested in finding ways of personifying problems in ways that do not perpetuate gendered stereotypes. But it is not easy! (Russell & Carey, 2003, p. 84)

Gender partnerships

Cheryl White:

Throughout the 1980s the feminist movement was also influencing men in our families, friendship networks, and in the broader professional field. Here in Adelaide, Rob Hall, Alan Jenkins, and Michael White, along with a range of other men, were in conversation around these issues and each took up the invitations and challenges from women to develop ways of working with men who have been violent to women (see Hall, 1994; Jenkins, 1990; White, 1992, 2011a).

The 1980s were a time when our local community, as women and men, sought to develop new forms of gender partnership. Just as white women, such as me, cannot sustain an acute awareness of white privilege without continuing collaboration and feedback from people of colour and/or Aboriginal colleagues, I really think that men cannot sustain an acute gender awareness without continuing feedback and collaboration with women.

As gender partnerships grew, new forms of practice to respond to the issue of men's violence were generated. Locally, Dallas Colley and Alison Newton's work with women survivors of domestic violence, Maxine Joy's work with survivors of childhood sexual abuse, and Amanda Kamsler's (1990) work with survivors of sexual violence were significant. (White, 2016, p. 64)

Genderqueer

Denoting or relating to a person who does not subscribe to conventional gender distinctions but identifies with neither, both, or a combination of masculine and feminine genders. Also used to describe a form of analysis/politics.

[See QUEER THEORY]

'Giving-it-back' practices

Borrowing from the Alcoholics Anonymous and Narcotics Anonymous traditions in a giving-it-back practice, I try to catch workers up on stories that are told about them being of use to clients. These fellowships believe that 'giving back' is a path to maintaining preferred change. Re-connecting with other workers, and catching them up on the differences they have made in the lives of the people we work alongside, is not just a nice thing to do: it is an ethical obligation. I invite teams to overtly engage with giving-it-back as a community-making practice. (Reynolds, 2011, p. 37)

h

Half memories

Apart from being timeless memories, dissociated memories are half memories. What is excluded from dissociated memory is an account of the person's response to what they were being subject to. People are not passive recipients of the traumas they are subject to. Even if they are powerless to significantly influence what they are being put through, or have no options for escaping the traumatic context, they take what steps are available to them to modify what they are being subject to in some small way, or to modify the effects of this trauma on their lives and identities. Not only are the details of these responses excluded from dissociated memory, but the foundations of these responses are also erased; that is, what it was that the person continued to accord value to through this experience, including their sentiment of living, and the practices of life associated with this sentiment of living. Put in other words, traumatic memories are half memories as they exclude an account of personal agency that would be in harmony with the persons' familiar and preferred sense of myself. (White, 2004b, p. 79)

[See FULL MEMORIES]

Hegemonic masculinity

A term proposed by RW Connell (1995) to describe the dominant form of masculinity in any particular culture at any particular historical time. Raewyn Connell contrasts hegemonic masculinity with a diversity of masculinities that non comply, reject or fall short of the dominant.

Heritage of achievement

[See USABLE PAST]

Heritage of resistance

In circumstances of generational inequity, injustice, and social suffering, community members often know all too well that their individual actions alone cannot guarantee the changes they would like to see. They may also be aware that the social changes they long for may not occur in their lifetime. These situations call for a particular sort of story 'to make spirits strong'. Sharon Welch (1990) has described a number of elements that she believes are 'essential to maintain resistance in the face of overwhelming odds' (p. 20). These include a 'redefinition of responsible action' and a 'grounding in community':

> *Responsible action does not mean one individual resolving the problems of others. It is, rather, participation in a communal work, laying the groundwork for the creative response of people in the present and in the future. Responsible action means changing what can be altered in the present even though a problem is not completely resolved. Responsible action provides partial resolutions and the inspiration and conditions for further partial resolution by others. It is sustained and enabled by participation in a community of resistance.* (Welch, 1990, p. 75)
>
> … Sharon Welch describes … 'a heritage of resistance' (Welch, 1990, p. 75), a heritage that is conveyed and transmitted with each re-telling. (Denborough, Wingard, & White, 2009, p. 27)

Collective narrative practices (Denborough, 2008) can be used to generate and sustain such a heritage of resistance.

Herstory

History viewed from a female or specifically feminist perspective.

Hetero-normativity

Heteronormativity (Warner, 1991) is the institutionalisation of what we've come to call heterosexuality. It includes not only the sexual relationships between born male-bodied/male-identified people and born female-bodied/female identified people, but also all the practices and values that have come to represent those relationships. Central to this privileged structure is the gender binary, the arbiter of all gendered relationships. (Tilsen & Nylund, 2010, p. 66)

Heterosexism

Is the set of beliefs that privilege heterosexuality, heterosexual relationships and cisgendered identities over non-heterosexual relationships and non-normative gender identities (Leonard, Mitchell, Patel, & Fox, 2008). Heterosexism provides the 'social backdrop' for homophobic and transphobic prejudices, violence and discrimination (Fileborn, 2012).
(Child Family Community Australia, 2017).

Heterosexist assumptions

One early impetus for the generation of narrative therapy was to create a therapy free of heterosexist assumptions, as articulated by Daphne Hewson (1993/2002) in the following 'wishlist':

> What would be different:
>
> - If no therapists made assumptions about a person's sexuality or the gender of their partner or the sexuality of the parents of their child clients?
> - If all therapists recognised that, no matter whether clients label themselves as homosexual or heterosexual, they are each likely to vary in their position on both the homo/hetero intimacy continuum and the homo/hetero sexuality continuum, and that these positions influence their lived experience?
> - If gays and lesbians didn't have to cover up social embarrassment when their therapist realises they had made an unjustified assumption about sexuality?
> - If gay and lesbian clients never had to desensitise or educate their therapists about their lives?
> - If no therapists ever tried to 'normalise' gay or lesbian clients by avoiding discussions of the impact of their sexuality on their lived experience?
> - If gay and lesbian clients felt free to explore their internalised homophobia with their therapists without fearing that their sexual orientation would be questioned?
> - If no therapists assumed sameness in the sexual behaviours and patterns of gay, lesbian, and heterosexual clients (for example, not using penis-based criteria for considering lesbian sexuality)?
> - If it was legally, occupationally, and personally safe for all gay and lesbian therapists to come out to their colleagues? (and to their clients?)

Heterosexist assumptions

(continued)

- If therapists presenting at conferences or workshops sometimes discussed their work with homosexual couples and had a consistent pattern of labelling the sexuality of all couples, not just 'homosexual couples'?
- If all therapists who have not identified about 1 in 10 of their adult clients as homosexual, asked themselves, 'Why?'
- If all therapists recognised that the ending of a gay or lesbian relationship has the same potential importance to each partner and to their children as the ending of a heterosexual marriage?
- If all therapists acknowledged to children and adolescents who have gay or lesbian parents that this influences their lives, rather than having it 'normalised'?
- If the role of the non-biological parent in gay and lesbian couples was fully acknowledged and appreciated by all therapists (and by the law)?
- If no therapists were affected by the dominant discourse that gay men are in some way responsible for AIDS?
- If all therapists asked gay clients about the impact on their life and their relationships of their losses of friends and lovers in the AIDS epidemic? (Hewson cited in White, 2016, p. 20)

This is an abridged version of the original wish list. Please note that the language we would use in a similar wish list today would be different than the language used above. A similar wishlist today would wish to acknowledge the experiences of all people marginalized on the basis of gender or sexual orientation, including lesbian, gay, bisexual, pansexual, asexual, transgender, queer, intersex, two-spirit, and all the rest of the spectrum of gender and sexual diversity.

Heterosexuality

The term heterosexual, or straight, refers to a monosexual attraction to the 'other' gender: men who are attracted to women, and women who are attracted to men. However it is worth remembering that, due to cultural heteronormativity, homophobia, and biphobia, many people who are attracted to the 'same' gender, or more than one gender, will say they are heterosexual. Also, if we take a more diverse understanding of sex, gender, and sexuality, many people's attractions and relationships may look straight from the outside but be experienced as pretty queer on the inside, for example those involving trans and non-binary people, those involving submissive men and/or dominant women, or feminine men and/or masculine women, and those involving a variety of sex practices. (Barker, 2018, p. 37)

Homonormativity

A term that describes the privileging of certain people or relationships within the queer community (usually cisgendered, white, gay men). This term also refers to the assumption that LGBTIQ+ people will conform to mainstream, heterosexual culture, for example by adopting the idea that marriage and monogamy are natural and normal.

Homophobia

This entry was written by Claire Nettle

Refers to negative beliefs, prejudices and stereotypes about people who are not heterosexual. Also the basis for actions against people who are not heterosexual and people who are perceived to not be heterosexual. Homophobia is also used to police hegemonic masculinity among men regardless of sexuality and perceived sexuality.

Honouring the little steps

Power To Our Journeys:

We are committed to the honouring of the so-called 'little steps' we take in life. These are the kinds of steps that so many people in this world overlook, and they include getting out of bed, having a shower, and caring for our lives in general. We will not allow this culture's overriding concern with control to take away our appreciation of these little sacraments of daily life. Instead, we will take pride in them, and in the process, take note of our specialness. (Brigitte, Sue, Mem & Veronika, 1997, p. 214)

[See POWER TO OUR JOURNEYS]

i

INCITE! Critical Resistance Statement

An influential statement issued by prison abolitionists and feminists of colour in North America that calls on social justice movements to develop strategies and analysis that address both state AND interpersonal violence, particularly violence against women. http://www.incite-national.org/page/incite-critical-resistance-statement

---

Insider knowledge

This entry was written by Claire Nettle

Insider knowledge is firsthand, material knowledge developed through lived experience. It is often disregarded because it lacks the formal characteristics of 'scientific knowledge' (Epston, 2014, p. 107) and other expert opinions, which are readily acknowledged and recorded. Both professional and insider knowledges are limited; however, they can work cooperatively to co-create new understandings.

Insider knowledge includes the particular and situated knowledge (Haraway, 1988) a person possesses about their own problem, including knowledge about ways to respond to a problem. This knowledge is often implicit, emerging during the exploration of subjugated storylines.

A focus on insider knowledge can counter normative and professional ideas about the nature of problems and how they should be responded to. It can invite curiosity about how the person experiences and views the problem, and how they would prefer to respond. Insider knowledges can be collective as well as individual, and recording and circulating these knowledges can generate further understanding, resonance and solidarity.

[See COLLECTIVE DOCUMENTS; INSURRECTION OF SUBJUGATED KNOWLEDGES]

Insurrection of subjugated knowledges

He [Michel Foucault] says that it's in the periphery, at the extremities, that these techniques of power become most available for our inspection… we can see these techniques operating in relationships between husbands and wives, in schools and clinics, and so on … He'd also argue that that's probably where they should be challenged, and he'd probably argue, I mean I don't know because he's not around anymore and I don't know how much he really talked about effective action, but he'd probably argue that it's very important that we challenge the techniques of power on the local level. And that his idea of a political program is not to be involved in a political party or be involved in some sort of insurrection or anything like that, his idea is to be involved in the local level helping people challenge the techniques of power and the subjugation to those techniques. And instead of the insurrection of persons, this is the insurrection of the subjugated knowledges, this is an insurrection of alternative knowledges … (White, 1989)

Intergenerational honouring

A term introduced by David Denborough (2010a) to describe narrative practices including definitional ceremonies that seek to redress intergenerational conflict. The concept has been particularly significant in work with migrant and refugee communities whose intergenerational relationships have been affected by racism.

[See: DEFINITIONAL CEREMONIES]

Intersectionality (and intersectional feminisms)

Kimberlé Williams Crenshaw (1989) introduced and developed the concept of intersectionality and intersectional theory to analyse the ways in which race and gender intersect in the lives of Black women, who then experience oppression that might come from multiple directions. This theory has since been expanded to explore how a wide range of interlocking or intersecting social identities, particularly subjugated identities, influence experiences of oppression, domination or discrimination in complex ways. Kimberlé Crenshaw's work led to the development of 'intersectional feminism', which examines the specific experiences of oppression and discrimination that women are subjected to due to the interwoven effects of inhabiting particular positions and identities, including those regarding ethnicity, sexuality, disability and class (see www.dulwichcentre.com.au/feminisms)

> Neither Black liberationist politics nor feminist theory can ignore the intersectional experiences of those whom the movements claim as their respective constituents. In order to include Black women, both movements must distance themselves from earlier approaches in which experiences are relevant only when they are related to certain clearly identifiable causes (for example, the oppression of Blacks is significant when based on race, of women when based on gender). The praxis of both should be centered on the life chances and life situations of people who should be cared about without regard to the source of their difficulties. (Crenshaw, 1989, p. 166)

Intersex people

Intersex people are born with physical or biological sex characteristics (such as sexual anatomy, reproductive organs, hormonal patterns and/or chromosomal patterns) that are more diverse than stereotypical definitions for male or female bodies. For some people these traits are apparent prenatally or at birth, while for others they emerge later in life, often at puberty … We recognise our diverse histories and use the word intersex inclusively, and acknowledging our right to self-determination …

We call for the immediate prohibition as a criminal act of deferrable medical interventions, including surgical and hormonal interventions, that alter the sex characteristics of infants and children without personal consent. We call for freely-given and fully informed consent by individuals, with individuals and families having mandatory independent access to funded counselling and peer support.

Regarding sex/gender classifications, sex and gender binaries are upheld by structural violence. Additionally, attempts to classify intersex people as a third sex/gender do not respect our diversity or right to self-determination. These can inflict wide-ranging harm regardless of whether an intersex person identifies with binary legal sex assigned at birth or not.

Intersex people

(continued)

Undue emphasis on how to classify intersex people rather than how we are treated is also a form of structural violence. The larger goal is not to seek new classifications but to end legal classification systems and the hierarchies that lie behind them. Therefore:

a. As with race or religion, sex/gender should not be a legal category on birth certificates or identification documents for anybody.

b. While sex/gender classifications remain legally required, sex/gender assignments must be regarded as provisional. Given existing social conditions, we do not support the imposition of a third sex classification when births are initially registered.

c. Recognising that any child may grow up to identify with a different sex/gender, and that the decision about the sex of rearing of an intersex child may have been incorrect, sex/gender classifications must be legally correctable through a simple administrative procedure at the request of the individual concerned.

d. Individuals able to consent should be able to choose between female (F), male (M), non-binary, alternative gender markers, or multiple options.

Extract from Darlington Statement, March 2017. Full statement available at: https://ihra.org.au/darlington-statement/

Investigative reporter (stance)

The form of inquiry that is employed during externalizing conversations can be likened to investigative reporting. The primary goal of investigative reporting is to develop an exposé on the corruption associated with abuses of power and privilege. Although investigative reporters are not politically neutral, the activities of their inquiry do not take them into the domains of problem-solving, of enacting reform, or of engaging in direct power struggles with those who might be perpetrating abuses of power and privilege. Investigative reporters are not usually 'hotly' engaged with the subjects of their investigations. Rather, their actions usually reflect a relatively 'cool' engagement.

In response to the investigative questions posed by the therapist, the people in therapy also assume an investigative-reporter-like position. In this way they contribute to building an exposé of the character of the problem, its operations and activities, and the purposes that inform these operations and activities. At this time, people are not encouraged to focus on efforts to resolve the problem, reform the problem, or engage in a direct struggle with the problem. (White, 2007, pp. 27–28)

Inviting people in

A supplementary metaphor (to 'coming out') developed by Sekneh Hammoud-Beckett (2007) and the LGBTQ+ young people of Muslim heritage with whom she works. The metaphor refers to imagining marginalized sexual orientations or gender experiences as a treasure chest, into which trusted people can be 'invited in' to share, rather than a restrictive closet which must be escaped.

Islamophobia

Young Muslim women are currently most vulnerable to public Islamophobia (hostility/discrimination directed at Muslims). To hear their stories of the ways they 'try not to take people's hate into their hearts', see: https://dulwichcentre.com.au/knowledge

j

i

Justice

The Power to Our Journeys Group wrote powerfully about the link between their experiences of hostile voices and visions (often diagnosed as schizophrenia) and issues of justice:

> It has been important for us to experience our work to reclaim our lives from the troublesome voices and visions as a struggle against injustice. These voices and visions are oppressive, and since our work on revising our relationship with these voices and visions addresses issues of power and control, then this relationship is a political relationship. This political understanding provides us with strength, as it keeps us in touch with the fact that we are not just on a personal journey, but also on a political journey.
> (Brigitte, Sue, Mem & Veronika, 1997, p. 208)

[See NARRATIVE JUSTICE; POWER TO OUR JOURNEYS]

Justice-doing

> If we embrace our work as justice-doing we will use our power as community workers and therapists to transform the social contexts of oppression. By this I mean work to change the real conditions of people's lives rather than helping them adjust to oppression. (Reynolds, 2011, p. 29)

Just Therapy

The Just Therapy Team from the Family Centre of Lower Hutt, New Zealand, has sought to create forms of practice that do not separate therapy from justice. They have also been influential in the development of partnerships across cultures and genders. (Waldegrave, Tamasese, Tuhaka & Campbell, 2003)

k

Katharsis

> Michael White: … I am using the word Katharsis in one of its most senior, or classical senses. I am not referring to the contemporary notion of catharsis which is considered an individual matter of discharging and one that views the emotional system as a part hydraulic/steam engine. I am referring to an earlier, classical idea of Katharsis, which refers to the experience one had when one witnessed a performance that was moving of them in some way, or when one was an audience to the expression of beautiful prose … (White, 2001)

According to the classical definition of katharsis:

> … an experience is kathartic if one is moved by it – moved not just in terms of having an emotional experience, but in terms of being transported to another place in which one might:
>
> - Achieve a new perspective on one's life and identity
> - Reengage with neglected aspects of one's own history
> - Reconnect with revered values and purposes for one's life
> - Make new meanings of experiences of one's life that were not previously understood
> - Experience a familiarity with knowledge of life and skills of living that one was previously barely aware of
> - Initiate steps in one's life otherwise never considered
> - Think beyond what one routinely thinks (White, 2007, p. 195)

Kaurna people

Dulwich Centre stands on the land of the Kaurna people, the Traditional Custodians of the Adelaide Plains.

Labels

… [It] is difficult to be in opposition to labels per se. In language, there is always naming, and so we always have labels of one sort or another. What is of critical importance, however, is the nature of the discourses that are associated with this naming: A consideration of discourse takes us to specific questions about any naming. What knowledges are privileged in a particular process of naming, and what knowledges are rendered irrelevant or are disqualified in this process? Who is qualified to speak and to name, and under what circumstances is it acceptable for them to do so? What relational practices and techniques of power are associated with acts of naming, of diagnosing and what are the real effects, on people's lives, of these practices and techniques? And so on. Here I have been trying to emphasise the extent to which it is discourse that is of vital consideration.

Of course, the labels associated with one discourse can be usurped by taking them up into alternative discourses. This is often achieved by marginalised groups. When these labels are taken up and inserted into an alternative discourse, they often become terms of pride, and ones that represent certain lifestyle choices and knowledges about ways of being and thinking. This has the effect of taking such labels a long way from the mainstream discourse that had been so subjugating of people in marginalised groups. (White, 1995b, pp. 119–120)

Landscape of action

Jerome Bruner (1986), borrowing significantly from the literary theorists Griemas and Courtes (1976), proposed that stories are principally composed of two landscapes – a 'landscape of action' and a 'landscape of consciousness'. The landscape of action is the 'material' of the story and is composed of the sequence of events that make up the plot (sjuzet) and the underlying theme (fabula). (White, 2007, pp. 77–78).

In re-authoring conversations, landscape of action questions invite people to link unique outcomes (events) through time, thus forming alternative plots:

- How did you get yourself ready to take this step? What preparations led up to it?
- Just prior to taking this step, did you nearly turn back? If so, how did you stop yourself from doing so?
- Looking back from this vantage point, what did you notice yourself doing that might have contributed to this achievement?
- Could you give me some background to this? What were the circumstances surrounding this achievement? Did anyone else make a contribution? If so, would you describe this?
- What were you thinking at the time? Have you been advising yourself differently? What did you tell yourself that pulled you through on this occasion?
- What developments have occurred in other areas of your life that may relate to this? How do you think these developments prepared the way for you to take these steps? (White, 1991, p. 30)

Landscape of consciousness (or landscape of identity)

> Jerome Bruner (1986) … proposed that stories are principally composed of two landscapes – a 'landscape of action' and a 'landscape of consciousness'. The landscape of consciousness is composed of 'what those involved in the action know, think, or feel, or do not know, think or feel' (Bruner, 1986, p. 14). This landscape features the consciousness of the protagonists of the story and is significantly composed of their reflections on the events of the landscape of action – of their attribution of meaning to these events, of their deductions about the intentions and purposes that are shaping of these events, and of their conclusions about the character and identity of the other protagonists in light of these events. (White, 2007, pp. 77–78)

In reauthoring conversations, landscape of identity questions invite people to reflect on:

> a) the nature of their preferences and their desires,
>
> b) the character of various personal and relationship qualities,
>
> c) the constitution of their intentional states,
>
> d) the composition of their preferred beliefs, and, lastly,
>
> e) the nature of their commitments. (White, 1991, p. 31)

Examples include:

- Let's reflect for a moment on these recent developments. What new conclusions might you reach about your tastes; about what is appealing to you; about what you are attracted to?
- What do these discoveries tell you about what you want for your life?
- How would you describe the qualities that you experienced in your relationship at this earlier time, when you managed to support each other in the face of adversity?
- What do these developments inform you about what suits you as a person? (White, 1991, p. 31)

'Language' of individualism / 'language' of tradition and collective commitment

… perhaps it is possible to consider that, within any culture, there is both a 'language' of individualism and a 'language' of tradition and collective commitment … In some contexts, some cultures, at different times in history, one of these languages may be spoken more loudly or more eloquently than the other. What's more, people within any culture move in and out of these languages constantly. There are also many different ways of speaking either a language of individualism or a language of collectivity …

There are a number of reasons why it may be significant for practitioners to develop conceptual tools to notice the different individualistic and socio-centric 'languages' at play in our work with individuals, groups and communities. Firstly, if we start to notice that those with whom we are working are wishing to speak not only on their own behalf but also to represent those affected by a particular social issue, then this can open new pathways for our conversations.

Secondly, and equally importantly, if we start to develop conceptual tools to notice individualistic and socio-centric ways of speaking, this may assist us to avoid imposing our own personal/cultural/gender bias, or replicating the dominant discourses of our culture, on those with whom we work. If we don't notice whether our conversations/actions are privileging a language of individualism over a sociocentric language (or vice versa) then we run the risk of replicating our language, our grammar, our speech patterns of the language of identity, onto others.

Therapeutic practice overwhelmingly listens to, attends to, and builds upon, individualistic speech. To do so, while paying less or no attention to collective speech patterns and their implications, seems hazardous. I am not suggesting we seek to impose 'collective practice' on those with whom we work, but instead to begin to notice, attend to, and build upon, collective speech patterns just as therapeutic practice conventionally builds upon individualistic speech. In this way, we can follow client speech patterns – both individualistic and collective – and see where they lead us. (Denborough, 2008, pp. 179–188)

Lateral violence (a conversation with)

Lateral violence is the name given to the harmful and undermining practices that members of oppressed groups can engage in against each other as a result of marginalisation. Aunty Barbara Wingard developed a collective externalising 'interview' with Lateral Violence. In this interview, Lateral Violence provides 'its own' exposé. Since its first publication (Wingard, 2010), this externalising script has been used to spark conversations in many communities about Lateral Violence, including in Woorabinda Aboriginal community. The special skills that Elders and young people from Woorabinda are using to respond to Lateral Violence have also been documented and shared (see Wingard, Johnson & Drahm-Butler, 2015).

League

David Epston and Stephen Madigan began to create networks of clients which they called 'leagues' so that they could provide consultation, information and support to each other. The best known example of such a league is the Anti-Anorexia/Anti-Bulimia League (Epston & Maisel, 2009; Grieves, 1997; Lock, Epston & Maisel 2004; Lock, Epston, Maisel & de Faria, 2005; Madigan, 2019; Maisel, Epston & Borden, 2004; Malson & Burns, 2009). The development of leagues was a key precedent for what is now referred to as collective narrative practice.

[See ANTI-ANOREXIA/BULIMIA LEAGUE, ARCHIVE. COMMUNITIES OF CONCERN]

'When labels are taken up and inserted into an alternative discourse, they often become terms of pride.'

Michael White

Lesbian / gay sexuality

> The words 'lesbian' and 'gay' refer to a monosexual attraction to the 'same' gender. Women who are attracted to women may use the word lesbian or gay, whereas men generally use the word gay. However, it is important to remember that due to biphobia, binary understandings of sexuality, and the non-binary and fluid way sex/gender works, some of those who identify as lesbian or gay do have some attraction to other genders. Some may experience this but feel a strong political or social affiliation to the lesbian and gay community. Also, there are many people who have same-sex attractions and activities who do not identify as lesbian or gay. This may be due to cultural homophobia or heteronormativity. Or it might be because they do not understand sexual attraction as dictating identity if they come from cultural contexts where this does not make sense, or have a more queer understanding. (Barker, 2018, pp. 35–36)

[See MONOSEXUAL]

Letter-writing campaigns

Stephen Madigan:

> Therapeutic letter writing campaigns assist people to re-remember lost aspects of themselves … Creating letter writing campaigns through communities of concern was a therapeutic means to counterbalance the issue of the problem saturated story and memory … Over the years, we have encouraged massive international writing campaigns that net literally hundreds of responses, and have had equally successful three-person problem blockades … The structure of campaign letters is usually the same. Together with the client I write a letter to selected members of the family/community (who the client and/or family member selects), and ask them to assist in a temporal re-remembering and witnessing process through lettered written accounts outlining their
>
> a) memories of their relationship with the client,
>
> b) their current hopes for the client, and
>
> c) how they anticipated their relationship growing with the client in the future. (Madigan, 2010; see also Madigan, 2019)

Liberative gender arrangements

Taimalieutu Kiwi Tamasese:

> We have tried to create an alternative way of approaching issues of gender and culture. This is a framework which focuses on the liberative traditions within all cultures. Within all our people's histories there are non-liberative as well as liberative stories, traditions and practices. As we have written about elsewhere, the principles of belonging, liberation and sacredness, and their inter-relationship, inform every aspect of our work. We're interested in playing our part to contribute to the traditions of belonging that are liberative, and that we could call sacred. Many sacred traditions are not liberative – so we do not make these our focus. And some liberative traditions don't emphasise belonging, so similarly we do not concentrate on these. We believe in creating contexts to further those traditions and practices in which belonging, liberation and sacredness meet. And we believe that this is a challenge for all peoples within our own cultures.
>
> What this has meant in terms of issues of gender and culture is that in order to address issues of gender justice we do not need to take an oppositional view of culture. Instead we are interested in tracing the liberative gender arrangements within a particular culture and finding ways that these traditional arrangements can inform our work. Let me describe this process in relation to Samoan culture.
>
> In order to find ways of grounding our current work on issues of gender in history, we thoroughly researched the traditions of gender arrangement within Samoan culture and by doing so unearthed liberative traditions. Specifically, our analysis of pre-colonised Samoa revealed a covenant relationship (feagaiga) between brother and sister that had the capacity to equalise the relationships between women and men. We learnt of traditional gender arrangements of partnership, and of the positions of respect that women had held within Samoan culture. This research was an involved process that we took very seriously. The fact that we can identify traditions within the culture that promote the sorts of gender relations to which we aspire has made our work in the present considerably easier. It has gone on to inform a range of projects within the Samoan community on issues of gender and culture that do not bring the two into opposition … And it has meant that as Samoan women we have been able to work on issues of gender without having our cultural identity questioned. (Tamasese, 2000, pp. 16–17)

Linking communities

A form of collective narrative practice involving groups and/or communities exchanging stories of the ways in which they have been responding to losses and injustices. In the process, previously unspoken skills and precious knowledge become richly known and new actions become possible (see Denborough, Koolmatrie, Mununggirritj, Marika, Dhurrkay & Yunupingu, 2006).

Listening teams

A term developed from the first narrative community gathering (Aboriginal Health Council, 1995) to explain the role of 'outsider witnesses':

> When people sat at the gathering they would choose which group or theme they wanted to discuss, and then they'd sit around and talk about this. The theme would be read out from the program, and then people would talk.
>
> While this was happening, listening teams made up of Aboriginal and non-Aboriginal workers trained in narrative approaches, would sit behind the group, listening and trying to keep notes of what people were saying. There'd be three or four of these listening team members for each group. Then we'd have a break, and the listening team would come into the middle of the circle and reflect back what they had heard.
>
> This meant that the families actually heard back the important parts of their own words. It wasn't until they heard this back from the listening teams that they could see how they had survived over the years. You could see families nodding, they were saying, 'It's actually been documented ... people have actually heard what we said'. And something would register for them for the first time.

'This reclaims the strengths of Aboriginal culture. Aboriginal culture has always had this. This has reiterated it, rejuvenated it.'

Participant at first narrative community gathering (Aboriginal Health Council)

Listening teams

(continued)

Then the listening teams would go back to their spots behind the group, outside the circle, and the family members would talk again, this time about what they'd heard reflected back from the listening teams. We'd hear people say, 'Well, I realise this is how we have survived all this … ' or 'why aren't I talking to my mum? Why aren't I talking to my brother?' We could see how extremely powerful it was for families to hear their own voices and their own words being reflected back to them. There was something about this that meant their own survival skills suddenly hit home to them.

A number of Aboriginal people commented that hearing their own stories reflected back in this way enabled them to see themselves differently, and to reclaim a pride in who they were. It also allowed them to recognise the remarkable strengths that they had demonstrated in surviving in the face of so much injustice. As one participant said about the listening groups, 'This reclaims the strengths of Aboriginal culture. Aboriginal culture has always had this. This has reiterated it, rejuvenated it. This is going on every day really around people's kitchen tables – so all you are doing now is going much wider and getting back to our culture. (Aboriginal Health Council, 1995, p. 19)

[See OUTSIDER WITNESS; DEFINITIONAL CEREMONY; NARRATIVE COMMUNITY GATHERING]

m

m

Man

Whether trans or cisgender, intersex or not, many people identify as men. However, what this means varies a great deal depending on their other intersecting attributes. It is important not to assume, for example, that being a man necessarily involves having a penis or being physically strong. (Barker, 2018, p. 26)

Maps

A metaphor utilised by Michael White to make transparent some of what was guiding his questions in therapy:

> Why maps? Well, on a personal level, I have always had a fascination with other worlds. I grew up in a working-class family in a mostly working-class community, and although access to other worlds of life was limited, I was always deeply curious about those worlds. When I was a young boy it was maps that made it possible for me to dream those other worlds up and imaginatively transport myself to other places.
>
> Then, on my 10th birthday, I received the gift of a bicycle. To this day I have never received another gift that meant as much to me as this bicycle (and to this day I cannot live without access to a bicycle). I now had means of visiting other worlds. Guided by maps, and in the company of my younger brother, our friends, and our dog, Prince, I would ride for whole days into the worlds that neighbored on my community – worlds that I became fascinated with but was barely able to touch the surface of. I can still recall my wonder on the occasion of first riding into a middle-class world that looked like the 'American dream' of the 1950s, one that had become familiar to me through radio and billboard

advertising and through the few magazines I had managed to get my hands on … My lifelong fascination for maps has led me to look at them as a metaphor for my work with people who consult me about a range of concerns, dilemmas, and problems. When we sit down together I know that we are embarking on a journey to a destination that cannot be precisely specified, and via routes that cannot be predetermined. I know that we will probably take some extraordinarily scenic routes to these unknown destinations. I know that as we approach these destinations we will be stepping into other worlds of experience.

The maps that I review in this book are, like any maps, constructions that can be referred to for guidance on our journeys – in this case, on our journeys with the people who consult us about the predicaments and problems of their lives. Like other maps, they can be employed to assist us in finding our way to destinations that could not have been specified ahead of the journey, via routes that could not have been predetermined. And, like other maps, the maps that I present in this book contribute to an awareness of the diversity of avenues that are available to preferred destinations, avenues that can be charted and rendered familiar. I have formulated these maps over the years principally in response to requests from others to render more transparent the therapeutic processes that I have developed. I will emphasize here that the maps of this book are not the maps of narrative practice or a 'true' and 'correct' guide to narrative practice, whatever narrative practice is taken to be.

As the author of these maps, it is important for me to emphasize that I do not use them to police my conversations with the people who consult me. Therapeutic conversations are not ordered, and I make no effort to determine my response to people's expressions ahead of these expressions. I am aware, however, that maps like those presented in this book help me to respond to people in ways that open opportunities for them to explore neglected aspects of the territories of their own lives. This provides people with avenues of possibility for addressing the predicaments and problems of their lives in ways that they wouldn't have imagined. (White, 2007, pp. 3–5).

Power to Our Journeys Group:

> We have all had a variety of experiences with medication, some of these satisfactory, some of them not. It is clear to us all that our experiences with medications become more satisfactory when we consider them to be tools for us, not ends in themselves. Drugs are tools that open space for us to work with others on the exposé of the troublesome voices and visions, on our friendships, and in the honouring of our knowledge of life. It is in this space that we can get our heads together. So, drugs can open up possibilities for us to take action to free ourselves from domination. However, it is of critical importance that we don't allow drugs to oppress us. We use drugs, but won't be used by them. (Brigitte, Sue, Mem & Veronika, 1997, p. 209)

Michael White (1995b):

> In regard to drugs, I have not taken a general position on the so called antipsychotic medications. Instead, I have been far more interested to find what is enabling for people in regard to this question – and here I am using the word 'enabling' in its positive sense. This consideration leads to specific questions:
>
> - How might one go about assisting people to determine whether these drugs are contributing to their quality of life, or whether they are subtracting from this?
> - How might one go about assisting people to determine in which ways these drugs might be enabling, and in which ways they might be disabling?
> - How might one go about assisting people to monitor the effects of different medications, and of different levels of these medications?
> - How might one go about assisting people to evaluate the real effects of these medications on their lives and in their relationships with others?

- How might one go about assisting people to establish what might be for them suitable criteria for such an evaluation?
- How might one go about assisting people to fully inform themselves about the various negative side-effects of these drugs?
- How might one go about assisting people to identify which people are most invested in compliance with regimes of medications, which people are least invested in this, and the particular interests of these parties?

> I do hope that this discussion goes some way towards challenging the view that I am opposed to the use of drugs. I have witnessed drugs being used in ways that have a profound effect in opening up the horizons of people's lives, in ways that bring a range of new possibilities for action. And I have also witnessed drugs being used in ways that are primarily for the purposes of social control, in ways that subtract very significantly from people's possibilities for action, in ways that dispossess people of choice. (White, 1995b, pp. 117–118)

[See POWER TO OUR JOURNEYS]

Metaphoric narrative practice

Approaches such as the Tree of Life, Team of Life, Kite of Life, were developed to enable people to address significant hardship or trauma they had experienced in ways that were not retraumatising.

> Significantly, metaphoric narrative practice doesn't require people to speak in the first person about the hardships. It enables meaning to be conveyed through metaphor rather than direct speech. (Denborough, 2018, p. 53)

Migration of identity

Michael White drew on the rites of passage metaphor (Victor Turner, 1969) to discuss journeys of change:

> This *Migration of Identity* journey is identified as having three stages of change. The first phase is described as the *separation* phase, in which a person lets go of their life as they know it. The second is the *liminal* phase where the way a person knows the world is questioned. The third is identified as the *reincorporation* phase, where one finds their new way of being. As one journeys through these phases, it is known as a migration of identity.' (Drahm-Butler, 2015, p. 39)

Michael White (1995c):

> If women who are working to leave and to stay out of relationships in which they are subject to violence by men appreciate the extent to which this project engages them in a 'migration of identity', and if they come to understand the processes involved in such migrations, then it becomes more possible for them to see this project through. The identity that women have experienced prior to the separation is one that has been imposed in so many ways by the man who is abusive of them, and, as well, by other persons who might have perpetrated abuse in their families of origin, and/or in some of the other institutions of this culture.
>
> Because achieving control of the woman is such an imperative for men who abuse, throughout their relationships with women they go about relentlessly and systematically reinterpreting these women's histories and identities. So, when women take steps to break free, they are doing a great deal more than breaking from the ongoing trauma, they are doing a great deal more than breaking from a familiar social network, and they are doing a great deal more than stepping into material insecurity – although all of this alone is more than enough to have to deal with at any time in one's life.
>
> At this time, women are also embarking on a migration of identity. And, in this migration, there is always some distance between the point of separation from the abusive context and the point of arrival at some preferred location in life, and at some alternative and preferred account of one's identity. There is always some distance between these two points in terms of time. And in this

Migration of identity

(continued)

> space, as in any migratory process, women characteristically go through a range of experiences, many of them difficult.
>
> In this 'liminal' or 'betwixt' and between' space, confusion and disorientation reigns, and often nothing seems manageable any more, not even one's relationship with one's children. It is in this space that women are vulnerable to a sense of total incompetence and personal failure, to feelings of desperation and acute despair.
>
> … If women have the opportunity to map their experience of the descent into this trough of confusion and disorientation as part of a process, if they have the opportunity to map this as a part of an ongoing journey, rather than interpret it as regress, then they are less at risk of turning back to an unchanged violent context. If women can understand these experiences as the products of a migration of identity, it becomes more possible for them to persevere with their journey despite the disorientation and the confusion. Such acts of mapping assist women to place their distress within the context of progress, to stand by and to hold onto the idea that the future might hold something different for them, to hold onto their hopes, to their expectations for a better life, to keep in sight the horizon of another world. (White, 1995c, p. 100)

The migration of identity concept is expanded upon by Palestinian narrative therapist, Nihaya Mahmud Abu-Rayyan, in her paper, 'The Seasons of Life: Ex-detainees reclaiming their lives' (2009):

> When we move from one stage of life to another, it can make all the difference if we use the expertise we developed on the first stage in order to face the difficult situations of the next. All that we learnt in autumn can assist us to deal with winter. All that we learnt during winter can help us throughout spring. And all that we learnt in spring can provide comfort during summer, and so on.
>
> Only when there is this sense of continuity can we look forward to life. And as the seasons cycle, we can then remember what we have passed through, how we have changed, and how we have remained the same.

Migration of identity *(continued)*

While meeting with ex-prisoners, the metaphor of the seasons of life provides continuity for those who have been through great hardship. It provides a chance for them to speak about the different stages or seasons that they have passed through and how what they learnt in one season can assist them in another. Significantly, this provides for conversations of pride, not shame.

We speak about the tough experiences and their profound struggles and also about their achievements and what they learned about life through time in prison. Importantly, we talk about the abilities and skills they developed in dealing with life in prison and how such approaches are able to assist them in their lives now. Often the person has not been conscious or aware of these abilities until our conversations. By finding ways to have these conversations we can build a sense of continuity between how they dealt with life in prison and how they might live their lives now. (pp. 25–26)

Misgendering

An occurrence where a person is described or addressed using language that does not match their gender identity (Ansara, 2013). This can include the incorrect use of pronouns (she/he/they), familial titles (father, sister, uncle) and, at times, other words that traditionally have gendered applications (pretty, handsome, etc.). For more information and ideas about ways of trying to prevent misgendering see: www.dulwichcentre.com.au/misgendering

[See PRONOUNS]

Misogyny

Dislike of, contempt for, or ingrained prejudice against women.

Modern power

Michael White:

For the past fifteen or so years I have had a strong interest in the analysis of modern systems of power. In this interest I have drawn principally on the work of Michel Foucault … a French historian of systems of thought. Over this time I have explored a range of implications of this analysis of modern power for therapeutic practice … When considerations of power are raised in the context of therapeutic explorations, invariably it is a classical analysis of traditional power that is evoked. This conceives of a power that is appropriated by certain individuals and groups; of a power that is taken up by these individuals and groups according to particular and unitary interests. This is a power that is understood to exist at a defined centre, and that is exercised from the top-down by those who have a monopoly on it. It is a power that is characterised as principally negative in its function; that is, it is a power that operates to oppress, repress, limit, prohibit, impose, and to coerce. This is a power that people are mostly subject to, not one that people generally participate in the exercise of. In contemporary times this version of power is often considered to be synonymous with the 'system' ('it's the system') that virtually everyone is on the outside of. In situating their lives, people routinely claim a position that is exterior to this power, regardless of whatever privilege they might have on account of where their lives are located in the domains of class, race, economics, and social advantage.

Foucault drew attention to the development of another version of power that exists in the shadows of these traditional operations of power. According to his studies, this is a distinct mechanism of modern power that has, over the last three hundred or so years, progressively displaced many of the operations of traditional power in the contemporary era of western culture. This modern power has now become the predominant system of power in the achievement of social control. This is a power that recruits people's active participation in the fashioning of their own lives, their relationships, and their identities, according to the constructed norms of culture – we are both a consequence of this power, and a vehicle for it. By this account, this is a system of power that is particularly insidious and pervasive. It is a power that is everywhere to be perceived in its local operations, in our intimate lives and relationships. Foucault sought to illustrate the many ways that we live our lives on the inside

'Upon first reading Foucault on modern power, I experienced a special joy ...'

Michael White

Modern power

(continued)

of the web of power relations of this system of modern power, and to draw attention to the extent to which we have become its unwitting instruments ... [U]pon first reading Foucault on modern power, I experienced a special joy ... If the operations of modern power are derived through the uptake of self and relationship practices that are first developed at the local level of culture, and if they principally operate at these levels – in clinics, schools, families, and so on – then there is the ever present potential for people to contribute to social change through the local development and sponsorship of self- and relationship-forming practices that do not directly reproduce the constructed norms of contemporary culture ...

If the professional disciplines have played a key role in the phenomenon of modern power, then the culture of therapy is positioned in the heartland of the development of its technology. This conclusion emphasises the small 'p' political aspects of therapeutic practice, and inspires us to work on the development of practices that are 'counter' to this technology when many of the problems that people present to therapists are derived through the operations of modern power. (White, 2002a, pp. 153–156)

Monosexism

Monosexism … refers to the structural privileging of monosexual identities and behaviours. So, monosexism refers, for example, to the belief that one can only be either straight or gay, that it is better to be monosexual than bisexual*, that only monosexual identities are 'real', that monosexual issues are the only ones deserving of attention, etc. Monosexism causes bisexual erasure (from media, literature, art, TV and film, etc.), it causes discrimination when it comes to activist priorities, budgeting, etc. It causes the social isolation that leads many bis* to have poor health and mental health, and prevents proper treatment and support that might help alleviate them. It keeps bi* people 'low' on the 'pecking order' and creates all sorts of oppression. I see monosexism as the main factor responsible for all the horrible statistics in the Bisexual Invisibility report, for example. So, basically, monosexism is the system, the base structure. It is everything which isn't directly aimed at bi* people but nonetheless has the effect of eradicating our existence or legitimacy. (Eisner, 2013)

Monosexual

Monosexuality is romantic or sexual attraction to members of one sex or gender only. A monosexual person may identify as heterosexual or homosexual. In discussions of sexual orientation, the term is used in contrast to bisexuality or pansexuality.

Morals

Michel Foucault: I was telling you earlier about the three elements in my morals. They are:

(1) the refusal to accept as self-evident the things that are proposed to us;

(2) the need to analyse and to know, since we can accomplish nothing without reflection and understanding – thus, the principle of curiosity; and

(3) the principle of innovation: to seek out in our reflection those things that have never been thought or imagined. Thus: refusal, curiosity, innovation. (Foucault, 1988c, p. 1)

'Mother-blame, what are you wanting to achieve in women's lives?'

Mother-blame

When working with groups of women, we have found that a light-hearted and useful way to make the operations of a discourse really clear is to have it enacted by one of us workers. The discourse gets played as an externalised 'character' by someone who knows a bit about the workings of that particular discourse, and this person is then interviewed by the group about its tricks and tactics. For example, in group work or community gatherings with mothers who have experienced violence, we have often interviewed 'Mother-blame'. We invite this 'special guest' along to the group and the group then proceeds to interview 'Mother-blame' as if the members of the group are investigative journalists. We ask questions that are designed to unmask the Mother-blame's intentions, tactics and ways of operating. We ask questions of Mother-blame such as:

- What are you wanting to achieve in women's lives?
- What are some of the ideas and beliefs that are around in our culture that support your work?
- What do you try to talk women into about themselves?
- Who are your friends and allies?
- What effects do you have on women's relationships with their children?
- What are your favourite tricks or tactics?'

'Mother-blame, is it a worry to know that women are starting to wise-up to you?'

Mother-blame
(continued)

We also explore the practices that can undermine the operations of Mother-blame:

- What can women do to resist you getting into their lives?
- What type of things might motivate women to get free from your clutches?
- What sorts of places are hardest for you to be around?
- What sorts of ideas might women have that really get up your nose?
- What's it like to talk about yourself in this way?
- Is it a worry to know that women are starting to wise-up to you?

Through these conversations with Mother-blame it quickly becomes apparent to the women in the group that they are not the only ones who have been influenced by this discourse. They are able to see Mother-blame for what it is – a set of unhelpful ideas and beliefs that have women believing that they are to blame for whatever is going on for their children, and for the violence to which the children have been subjected. Interviewing the discourse in this way can be very effective in breaking the silence and secrecy that surrounds Mother-blame. (Russell & Carey, 2003, pp. 76–77; see also Freer, 1997)

[See DISCOURSE; EXTERNALISATION]

n

n

Naming injustice

Naming Injustice was the name of one of the themes in the program for the first narrative community gathering (for Aboriginal families who had lost a loved one in custody):

> *Naming injustice*
>
> Many of the deaths of Aboriginal people are connected to past and present injustices. This makes it harder for relatives and friends to get through the grief. This can leave people with self-blame, self-hate, self-neglect, confusion, depression and stress. Getting through the grief is very important because this frees people from all of these negative experiences. When grief is made worse by injustices, it is very important to name these injustices, and to name how these injustices were done – to name the methods of these injustices. This naming helps people to get through the grief.
>
> To break free of the self-blame, self-hate, self-neglect, confusion, depression and stress, it is very important to name these injustices and methods in ways that are heard by other people. For other people to be there at this time makes a very big difference.
>
> You are invited to join in the work on grief by coming to one of these Naming Injustice groups. (Aboriginal Health Council, 1995, p. 6)

'We never separate healing from justice. These go hand-in-hand.'

Ibuka Counsellors

Narrative justice

This entry was written by Claire Nettle

Narrative therapy defends people's rights to name their own experiences, to define their own problems, and to honour the ways that their skills, abilities, relationships, history and culture can contribute to reclaiming their lives from the effects of hardship. Justice for people whose human rights have been violated includes the right to tell their own stories in their own ways. See: https://dulwichcentre.com.au/narrative-justice-and-human-rights/

The counsellors of Ibuka in Rwanda describe narrative justice in this way:

> We never separate healing from justice. These go hand-in-hand. We see in our work how justice is a form of healing and how healing is a form of justice. (Ibuka Counsellors quotes in Denborough, 2010b, p. 9)

[See CHARTER (DRAFT) OF STORYTELLING RIGHTS, STORYTELLING RIGHTS]

Narrative therapy as political activity

> If we accept Foucault's proposal that the techniques of power that 'incite' persons to constitute their lives through 'truth' are developed and perfected at the local level and are then taken up at the broader levels, then, in joining with persons to challenge these practices, we also accept that we are inevitably engaged in a political activity. (We would also acknowledge that, if we do not join with persons to challenge these techniques of power, then we are also engaged in political activity.) This is not a political activity that involves the proposal of an alternative ideology, but one that challenges the techniques that subjugate persons to a dominant ideology. (White & Epston, 1990, p. 29)

Narrative timeline

We were first introduced to the use of collective timelines through the Highlander Research and Education Center, where they have been used as a methodology of popular education for many years. Historically, workers at Highlander invited participants in workshops to speak about their 'Seeds of fire' (see Adams & Horton, 1975; Horton, J. Kohl, & H. Kohl, 1998; Jacobs, 2003). These were the moments in the participants' lives when the spark to contribute to broader social change first occurred. People were invited to name the date this occurred, to write this and a short story associated with the particular event on a card, and then place this on a broader collective timeline that had been mapped out around the room where the workshop was taking place. Often, a parallel timeline was also spoken about and depicted, this being the broader timeline of whatever issue people were meeting together to try to address. For instance, if the group was meeting in relation to labour relations, then a history of the labour movement might be depicted on one timeline, while the collective timeline created from participants' stories would run parallel to this around the room … In the mid-1990s, Cheryl White visited Highlander outside Knoxville, Tennessee, and was so impressed with the effectiveness of collective timelines that she encouraged me and others to explore their use in our work contexts. (Denborough, 2008, p. 144)

Needs

What Foucault proposes in his ideas of an ethics of the self is that one does not attempt to discover one's hidden needs, but rather one attempts to self-consciously deconstruct what are perceived as needs in order to discover new areas of experience … it is necessary to adopt an analytical approach which focuses not on needs but on discourses of needs. In other words, a politics of need interpretation. (McNay, 1992, p. 106)

Neoliberalism

The dominant political discourse around the world since the 1980s in which the primary metaphor has been the 'market'. Everything, including therapy, has been transformed into a marketplace and concepts like service and justice have been left to fend for themselves in competition with concepts of efficiency.

Wendy Brown:

> I treat neoliberalism as a governing rationality through which everything is 'economized' and in a very specific way: human beings become market actors and nothing but, every field of activity is seen as a market, and every entity (whether public or private, whether person, business, or state) is governed as a firm … Neoliberalism construes even non-wealth generating spheres – such as learning, dating, or exercising – in market terms, submits them to market metrics, and governs them with market techniques and practices. Above all, it casts people as human capital who must constantly tend to their own present and future value. (Wendy Brown in Shenk, 2015)

Neo-liberal fatalism

Cheryl White (2016) describes how Paulo Freire introduced her to the concept of neo-liberal fatalism during a meeting in São Paulo, Brazil.

> In 1997, the Landless Movement (Movement Sem Terra) held huge marches across Brazil. I was there to document hopeful approaches to working with homelessness, and had the opportunity to join these marches for a short time. In the process, we made connections with colleagues of Paulo Freire and after a phone call or two, we found ourselves generously invited to his home. As it turned out, this was to be Paulo Freire's final interview, which gave his words an added poignancy. With twinkling eyes, Freire railed against the ways in which the privileged in the world routinely look for solutions in the wrong places and then, when they cannot find the solutions there, they feel despair, and become convinced that broader change is not possible and therefore not worth aspiring to or acting towards. He introduced this phenomenon to us as 'neo-liberal fatalism'. As we left his home, his challenges were ringing in our ears and they still are, nineteen years on: How can we resist neo-liberal fatalism? How can we look for the solutions in the right places? How can we respond to stories of social suffering in ways that not only alleviate individual sorrow, but also address in some way broader injustices, violence, and abuses? (pp. 12–13)

Non-binary

Non-binary is an umbrella term for people who do not experience themselves as male or female (in the US the umbrella term genderqueer is more commonly used). As with 'man' and 'woman' this term is a big umbrella covering a wide range of different experiences, including people who:

- Do not have a gender (e.g. agender, gender neutral)
- Feel partially male or female (e.g. demi boy/girl)
- Are both masculine and feminine (e.g. bigender)
- Are located somewhere between male and female (e.g. androgynous)
- Have an additional – or third – gender,
- Move between genders (e.g. gender fluid)
- Reject the western binary gender system (e.g. genderfuck*) (Barker, 2018, p. 27)

[See GENDERQUEER; GENDER FLUID, GENDER IDENTITY]

Non-essentialist understandings

Non-essentialist understandings are a challenge to the modern idea that there is a self that is at the centre of who we are (White, 2000b, p. 106).

[See ESSENTIALISM]

Normalisation

This entry was written by Claire Nettle

Foucault (1975) used the term normalisation to describe the social construction of ideas and actions as 'normal', 'correct' and 'natural', and the penalising or pathologising of things that deviate from these ideals. This form of 'disciplinary power' is a means of social control.

> The normalizing tendencies of modern technologies of power are obscured behind the screen of individualization. The endless examination of one's inner self, which Foucault sees as a dominant characteristic of modern society, does not lead to greater self-knowledge, but rather is the result of a forgotten coercion. The obvious example of this is Foucault's famous attack on psychoanalysis. (McNay, 1992, p. 86)

[See MODERN POWER; PRODUCTIVE POWER]

Open non-monogamies

As with the other relationship styles and structures, there are a wide variety of ways of being openly, or consensually, non-monogamous. Common models are open relationships and polyamory.

Open relationships involve couples who have sexual – but not love – relationships with other people. For example, swingers have open relationships where they have sex with others in a social way, often at parties or clubs, either together or separately ...

Polyamory, or poly, involves people having multiple love relationships which can also be sexual. For example, some individuals have two equal relationships (a V arrangement where they are the bottom point on the V). Some form a triad, quad, or family of people who are all are involved with each other. (Barker, 2018, p. 49).

Orientalism

'Orientalism' is a way of seeing that imagines, emphasizes, exaggerates and distorts differences of Arab peoples and cultures as compared to that of Europe and the U.S. It often involves seeing Arab culture as exotic, backward, uncivilized, and at times dangerous. Edward W. Said, in his groundbreaking book, Orientalism, defined it as the acceptance in the West of 'the basic distinction between East and West as the starting point for elaborate theories, epics, novels, social descriptions, and political accounts concerning the Orient, its people, customs, "mind", destiny and so on.' (Arab American National Museum, 2011; see also Said, 1978)

Outsider witness A term drawn from the work of Barbara Myerhoff (1982; 1986), who used it to highlight the significance of audience responses to people's identity claims: that it is through the responses of 'outsider-witnesses' that our claims for our identities are authenticated. This is particularly significant for those facing invisibility and marginality:

> Definitional ceremonies deal with the problems of invisibility and marginality; they are strategies that provide opportunities for being seen and in one's own terms, garnering witnesses to one's worth, vitality and being. (Myerhoff 1986, p. 267)

Michael White developed particular ways of shaping outsider-witness responses:

> A key part of outsider witness retellings is their adherence to a tradition of acknowledgment ... Specifically, these retellings are not about giving affirmations, offering congratulatory responses, pointing out positives, focusing on strengths and resources, making moral judgments or evaluating people's lives against cultural norms (whether these judgments and evaluations are positive or negative), interpreting the lives of others and formulating hypotheses, delivering interventions with the intention of resolving people's problems, giving advice or presenting moral stories or homilies, re framing the events of people's lives, imposing alternative stories about people's lives, trying to help people with their predicaments and dilemmas, or expressing worry for the lives of others. Further, outsider witness responses are not so much about empathy and sympathy but about resonance – outsider witness responses that are most effective are those that represent what people give value to in a way that is highly resonant to these people. (White, 2007, pp. 187–188)

Outsider witness

(continued)

Cheryl White emphasises the responsibilities of people to also act differently as a result of witnessing the stories of others:

> These days, it seems that outsider-witness responses are often very respectful, but kind of 'sweet' and watered down, whereas in the early days they were also linked to a responsibility to act differently as a result of witnessing particular stories. For instance, when Michael White was working with people with diagnoses of schizophrenia, and trainees were acting as outsider-witnesses, these trainees would witness the courage with which those who were hearing voices were resisting or challenging the degradations of the psychiatric system. There would be an expectation that if trainees, well-paid middle class professionals, witnessed such courage and integrity, that they would learn from this, and commit to raising issues and contributing to transforming the mental health system, and not leave it only to people hearing voices to do so. Outsider-witness responses therefore included a link to social actions in addition to personal resonance or response. (White, 2016, p. 24)

[See: DEFINITIONAL CEREMONIES; LISTENING TEAMS]

p

q

Pacifying women

In my work as a therapist, how can I ensure that I am not pacifying women? Women's anger can be a vital force for broader social change. How can I ensure that I am not promoting individual solutions when the anger and the energy of the women consulting me could, with collective engagement, be harnessed and directed towards creating broader social change? How can I ensure in my work that I am not offering only individual comfort but am linking women's lives to other women's lives around shared purposes and shared actions?

At the same time, if in my conversations with women they do express anger, resistance or outrage at certain experiences in their life, how can I respond to this anger in ways that lead to preferred outcomes for the women concerned? How can I keep in check with those consulting me regarding their evaluation of the sorts of conversations we are sharing? (Russell & Carey, 2003, p. 84)

Pansexual

An individual whose sexual and/or romantic attraction to others is not restricted by gender. A pansexual person may be sexually and/or romantically attracted to any person, regardless of their gender identity.

Parrhesia

… Foucault's idea of 'parrhesia', or an oppositional practice of free speech, resembles his earlier notion of 'disqualified' or 'subjugated knowledges'. By this, Foucault means the discourses and experiences of subordinate and marginalized groups which, by never being fully articulated, have been denied official status. Examples of subjugated discourses are the knowledge of those who undertake psychiatric treatment, of homosexuals, of women, of children, etc. It is the task of genealogical history to carry out a 'tactical reversal' of these discourses, to activate them, into a resistant counterpower.
(McNay, 1992, p. 136)

Partnerships across gender and culture

Taimalieutu Kiwi Tamasese (2000):

> … we have developed partnerships across issues of culture and gender within the Family Centre (see Tamasese & Waldegrave 1996; Tamasese, Waldegrave, Tuhaka & Campbell 1998) … These are partnerships that are based on values of humility, respect, sacredness, reciprocity and love. They are also based on structures of accountability through caucusing, and leadership within these caucuses, that seek to protect against gender and culture bias in our day-to-day work. The Maori and Pacific island sections are self-determining, while the Pakeha (white section) runs its own affairs but is accountable to the other two sections. Similarly the women and the men caucus separately at times to address their own issues. As with the cultural work, we have found it helpful to agree to creative forms of accountability that address our gendered histories and consequent biases. The women's work is self-determining. The men manage their own responsibilities but are accountable to the women.
>
> What I will mention here is what these partnerships, these relationships, mean to me. Our partnerships and the structures of these partnerships have meant that we are not constantly locked into an oppositional frame. The partnerships provide space for separate men's and women's discussions, and for separate cultural caucuses. In these separate spaces groups are actively involved in the deconstruction and the reconstruction of gender and cultural traditions. The caucuses are also places where sustenance and support can be found in ways that further the partnerships.

'These are partnerships that are based on values of humility, respect, sacredness, reciprocity and love.'

Taimalieutu Kiwi Tamasese

Partnerships across gender and culture

(continued)

For me to be able to spend my life working on issues of gender and culture requires these long-term relationships. I need the ongoing relationships with men and with people of other cultures at The Family Centre in order to be able to move into the outside world and address issues of culture and of gender. These relationships sustain me. Sometimes there are difficulties but we all know that these are long-term committed relationships to one another. We know that in time the difficulties will be sorted out …

These partnerships are urgently needed. Throughout the world, women and men from Indigenous cultures and from less developed countries are creating lives severely restricted by the effects of racism and grossly unjust distribution of resources. Women from these cultures are also affected by marginalisation on the basis of their gender. It is the responsibility of every discipline to address these injustices, and the responsibility of each of us within them to play a part. Creating working partnerships across culture and gender is one way forward. (Tamasese, 2000, pp. 18–21)

Pathologising

> There now exists a simply fantastic number of opportunities that are available to mental health professionals for the pathologising of people's lives. Due to an extraordinary investment in the development of the discourses of pathology, we now have at our disposal a vast array of ways of speaking with and interacting with people that reproduce the subject/object dualism that is so pervasive in the structuring of relations in our culture.
>
> These ways of speaking and interacting with people puts them on the other side of knowledge, on the outside. These ways of speaking and acting make it possible for mental health professionals to construct people as the objects of psychiatric knowledge, to contribute to a sense of identity which has 'otherness' as its central feature. The success of these discourses is beyond question, and I believe that this achievement represents one of the truly great marginalisations of contemporary culture. (White, 1995b, pp. 112–113)

Pathologising discourses have the potential to bring to us a degree of comfort in a world in which it is becoming increasingly difficult to find this. These discourses make it possible to define those problems for which people seek help as aberrations. As such, they assist us to avoid the acknowledgement of the fact that these problems are very significantly of our culture, that these problems are products of our modes of life and of thought. The discourses of pathology make it possible for us to ignore the extent to which the problems for which people seek therapy are the outcome of certain practices of relationship and practices of the self, many of which are actually informed by modern notions of 'individualism'. And the discourse of pathology makes it possible for us to ignore the extent to which the problems for which people seek help are so often mired in the structures of inequality of our culture, including those pertaining to gender, race, ethnicity, class, economics, age, and so on.

Pathologising
(continued)

> If we can see the difficulties for which people seek help as the outcome of some aberration rather than a product of our ways of thought and ways of life, we can avoid facing our complicity in the maintenance of these ways of life and of thought. This assists us to disavow our complicity in the constitution of the worlds we share with others. In obscuring this link between the problems for which people seek help and the modes of life and thought of our culture, we can avoid facing the responsibility that we have to take action to address the context of people's lives, and we can avoid facing the responsibility that we have to dismantle the various structures of inequality that are associated with these. (White, 1995b, pp. 115–116)

[See NORMALISATION]

Patriarchal power

This entry was written by Claire Nettle

Patriarchal power is a pattern in which men, and things that are classified as masculine, dominate, oppress and exploit other people and things that are classified as feminine. Discourses justifying these patterns of power naturalise patriarchy and normalise fixed notions of masculinity as superior, often drawing on ideas of sex difference: 'Patriarchal power rests on the social meanings given to biological sexual difference' (Weedon, 1987, p. 2). Patriarchal power is embedded in social, cultural, economic and legal structures, and manifest in interpersonal relationships. Patriarchal power shapes relationships among men, as well as those between men and women.

Personal is political

[See CONSCIOUSNESS-RAISING; DECONSTRUCTION]

'It's important to understand that these ideas have been developed and constructed in history and in culture. If we understand that, we're not chained to the ideas, we're not tied to them. We can think outside of them.'

Michael White

Personality disorders

Personality disorders seem to be stacked against women in part because of the DSM [Diagnostic and Statistical Manual of Mental Disorders] …, the manual used to diagnose and treat mental health problems. Psychologist Marcie Kaplan made this point by inventing two fictitious personality disorders based on stereotypically male traits:

- Independent Personality Disorder – puts work and career above personal relationships, travels a lot and works long hours, makes career decisions without considering others' needs, is unable to express emotions.
- Restricted Personality Disorder – appears to be self-assured, shows limited emotional expression, resists answering others' emotional needs, is stoic.

But these male behaviors would not be diagnosed as 'disorders'. Masculinity is not clinically suspect; femininity is. (Marcie Kaplan, 1983, p. 791 cited in Kramarae & Treichler, 1985, p. 334)

A lot of people who have been through a lot of abuse and they've been isolated in this, wind up with a diagnosis of borderline personality disorder. This diagnosis obscures more than it reveals. (White, 2001)

Personal properties

How many of you have resources, personal resources? These have been around for longer than psychological needs; they've been around for a couple of hundred years or so. It's been a growing development . . . The whole idea that we have these personal properties is associated with the development of modern liberal theory. Liberal theory provides the basis of the Western democratic state . . . one of the cornerstones of liberal theory was . . . the recognition and preservation of the individual's right to own property, to possess property. It also preserved the individual's right to capitalise on their property . . . by mining it, and to bring to the surface these resources, or by cultivating their property to improve its assets. Now around the same time, there was this new idea that maybe . . . we have a self that's like personal property that we can own in the same way that we can own actual property: land. And so we can actually mine the self to discover the resources and to bring those resources to the surface, and to put them into circulation. So how many internal miners are there in this group? How many of you have found yourself in situations where you had to dig deep, to get in touch with your resources and to put them into circulation? Internal miners in the group? [laughter]

. . . And how many internal farmers are there in the group? How many of you have been into self-cultivation? The cultivation of the self? Cultivating this quality or this asset? So you're the internal farmers of the group . . .

These are relatively new understandings . . . this is all part of a tradition that . . . is often referred to as structuralist. Action in life as a surface manifestation of some element or essence that comes from the centre of who we are. And these ideas are now taken for granted. It's just naturally assumed that action is the surface manifestation of strengths, resources, psychological needs, relationship dynamics and so on . . . That is almost never questioned.

Now, I'm not saying that they're bad ideas, is that clear? I think some of those ideas are very beautiful ideas. But I think it's important to understand that these ideas have been developed and constructed in history and in culture. If we understand that, we're not chained to the ideas, we're not tied to them. We can think outside of them. (White, 2018)

Place

Mark Trudinger, in an influential paper considering the role of 'place' in narrative therapy (Trudinger, 2006), poses the following environmental questions and challenge to family therapists:

> Family therapy, while engaging with challenges posed by the inequalities and power relations of gender, race, class, sexuality, and so on, has been conspicuously silent on issues of the environment (Kidner 1996). Considerations of ideas of place and space often lead to reflecting on the broader 'natural' environment, and render environmental problems and issues – and people's concerns for them – more visible. In this context, engaging with ideas of place may be an entry point for therapists to take up environmental ethics in their work.
>
> People live in a broader environment than the usually-considered contexts of social and family relations; they live in relation to that environment; and are very much dependent on that environment, which, in most parts of the world, currently faces great peril. The broader 'culture of consumption', so often implicated in therapists' writings and practice about addiction and anorexia, also has massive environmental impacts that affect the lives of everyone on the planet. Environmental concerns are implicated in many of the more common 'illness narratives' that therapists attend to – such as the rise of asthma with the increase of the burning fossil fuels, and cancer with chemical manufacture.

Place

(continued)

> While narrative practice usually does not take up issues of etiology, it does concern itself with context. How might it be possible to avoid the problematic quagmires that can come with trafficking in etiology, while still being available to the very real effects of the multiple contexts of environmental issues in people's lives? How can we engage with nature without being 'naturalistic'? How might we be able to address the environmental impacts of our therapeutic and community workplaces and events? And what might happen if we were more attuned to considerations of the environment when attending to the 'territories' of people's lives? (Trudinger, 2006, p. 16)

Mary Heath (Personal communication, 21st February 2019):

> Reading Indigenous authors, in particular Irene Watson and Ward Churchill -- and working on Indigenous led campaigns -- has made me realise that casting place as environment has a politics of its own. Place is then not cast as Mother (or other relative or ancestor); we care for it rather than it caring for us; environment is the issue and not sovereignty, law or right relationship. As Irene Watson states: 'The future of the natural world, along with First peoples, could be secured by the state engaging in a process of de-colonisation.' (Watson, 2014, p. 518)

Place (and environmental action)

Within narrative practice, it can be significant to explore how our work can strengthen people's relationships to special places/environments that have contributed to their lives (Trudinger, 2006). Having done so, it then becomes possible to enable people to make contributions back to these places. I (David Denborough) have listed here various lines of enquiry that can assist in this process. These conversations can take place with individuals or collectives:

Historical places of sustenance

- During the course of your life have there been any particular places that have assisted you in dealing with the effects of difficulties in your life? These could be places of comfort, sustenance or reflection; they could be calming, generative, renewing or exhilarating places – places where the effects of whatever you were going through at the time were somehow lessened.

- Can you describe this place … its colours, sounds, textures and shades?

- What is the history of your relationship with this place, this land? How were you introduced to it? Which aspects of this history are yours alone and which have been shared with others?

- What is it about this place, and/or your relationship with it, that has made a difference to your life?

- What did you do in this place? How did you relate to it? What did the relationship consist of?

- Can you say more about what sort of difference it made to be in this place, or to remember your times there? How has this assisted you through difficult times?

- Are there other people who also found/find this place significant?

- Have there been times when you (or others) have also made a contribution to this place? Ways in which you and/or others have cared for it, protected it, sustained it, as it has you?

- If so, how did you do this? How did you learn to care for a place in this way?
- What sort of footprint did you leave in this place (this may be a physical 'footprint' or it may be certain memories that you left there)?

Current places of sustenance

- Are there any places that you visit now, that you currently relate to, that have some of the same characteristics as this place from your past? Are there any current traces of this past relationship to place that continue in your present life? [If so, then it becomes possible to ask the same sorts of questions listed above in relation to the present place, eg. describing the place, its significance, what they do there, the effects of this, history of relationship and so on …]

Turning to places of sustenance at this time of difficulty

- What might it mean for you at this current time of difficulty if you re-visited these places (in person or in memory)?
- Is there some way that this place could assist you in dealing with the current situation you are facing?
- Who might you take with you (in person or in memory) to re-visit this place?
- What would you do if you visited? Are there ways you would want to somehow convey to the place what it has meant to you in the past, and what you have been going through lately?
- If you could speak with this place now, what is it you might say?

Hazards facing places of sustenance

- Are there any hazards or threats now facing your special place(s) of the past or present? Or other places like these?
- If so, what are these hazards? What effects are these having on the place itself, and on those who may visit?

Place (and environmental action) *(continued)*

- Are there any ways in which you (and others) could make a contribution to the nurturing of this place? Could there, in the present, be a two-way relationship between you and this place? If so, what might this look like?
- If this was possible, would this in anyway assist you in dealing with the current difficult times you are facing? How?
- What sort of footprint would you like to leave at this place?

These sorts of lines of enquiry seek to honour people's relationship to land and significant places. They seek to richly story these relationships in ways that emphasize a mutuality of contribution in the hope that this creates a context by which this relationship may provide sustenance to people and to land. When these explorations are done with a collective, it's possible to visually represent the places of significance to those in the group. It may then be possible to develop collective projects of sustenance and regeneration. During the course of these projects that include environmental action it is possible to continually 'story' the actions that people are taking in relation to their history of connectedness to land and place. (For more about place in narrative therapy see Trudinger, 2006)

Political task

Michel Foucault: It seems to me that the real political task in a society such as ours is to criticise the workings of institutions, which appear to be both neutral and independent; to criticise and attack them in such a manner that the political violence which has always exercised itself obscurely through them will be unmasked, so that one can fight against them. (Chomsky & Foucault, 1974/2011, p. 49)

Politics in therapy

> At times I have … been asked to join debates about whether or not it is the therapist's place to bring politics to therapy. My standard response to such invitations is that, according to its terms, the debate is irrelevant and presumes a certain arrogance; that it is never a matter of whether or not we bring politics into the therapy room, but whether or not we are *prepared to acknowledge* the existence of these politics, and the degree to which we are prepared to be complicit in the reproduction of these politics. How could the therapeutic context possibly be exempt from the politics of gender, race, and class? How can therapy be exempt from the politics associated with the hierarchies of knowledge and the politics of marginalization in this culture? When people walk into the therapy room, they bring with them the politics of their relationships. And when people walk into a therapy room, they walk into a context that is structured by politics. (White, 2011b, p. 50)

This recognition leads to the following challenges:

- What can we build into the therapeutic context that might contribute to our awareness of the politics of relationship?
- How do we propose to deal with the political dilemmas raised in this work?
- What steps can we take to avoid being wholly complicit in the reproduction of the dominant social order?
- What are some of the necessary conditions of a therapy that is sensitive to the politics of gender, heterosexual dominance, race, culture, class, and sexual orientation?
- How might we go about interacting with persons in ways that assist them to identify, to embrace, and to honor their resistance to those acts of self-government that they are incited to engage in by the dominant knowledges and practices of power in this modern culture?
- How might we go about subverting the hierarchies of knowledges that privilege professional knowledge claims and open up new possibilities for dissent?

Politics in therapy
(continued)

- What possibilities are available to us for privileging alternative knowledges and the knowledgeableness of those persons who seek our help?
- How might we successfully confront ourselves with the moral and ethical responsibilities that we bear for the real effects of, or consequences of, our interactions with those persons who seek our help?
- What choices do we have in establishing structures that make our work accountable to those persons who seek our help – structures of accountability that might expose the real and the potential abuses in the practice of therapy?
- What are the appropriate ways for us to acknowledge the imbalance of power that is inherent in the therapeutic relationship?
- What actions can we take to mitigate the toxic effects of the imbalance of power that is inherent in the therapeutic relationship?
- How might we go about acknowledging our own location in the worlds of gender, race, class, culture, and sexual identity?
- And how might we go about acknowledging the implications of this location? (White, 2011b, pp. 53–54)

A wide range of therapists, including Aboriginal narrative practitioners, are rigorously and creatively engaging with contemporary politics in therapy (see for example: Wingard, Johnson & Drahm-Butler, 2015; Dowse, 2017; Lainson 2016; Sostar, 2018; and https://dulwichcentre.com.au/feminisms-project/)

Polyamory

The philosophy or state of being, or being open to being, in love or romantically involved with more than one person at the same time.

[See OPEN NON-MONOGAMIES]

Positively implicating parents

A way of enabling children to be on reasonable terms with their own history:

> There is a tradition within the field of psychotherapy of negatively implicating parents in children's lives. In other words, whenever a child displays some action that is deemed undesirable, the parent or care-givers are routinely seen to be implicated in this. This tradition of negatively implicating parents often has negative effects for both parents and children. It can have the effect of dividing the child from the parents, reinforcing a sense of incompetency for parents, and it makes it more difficult for the child to be on reasonable terms with their own history.
>
> As an antidote to this, there are many ways in which parents can be implicated positively in their children's expressions of skills and knowledge of life. This is possible even when there are aspects of the parents' management of child-rearing responsibilities that are potentially or actually traumatising. Of course, if a child is being traumatised by their parents, this must be acknowledged and addressed. This is always given priority. However, efforts to address these potentially or actually negative aspects of the parents' actions can be facilitated through implicating the parents positively in aspects of their children's expressions of life …
>
> It is possible to engage in conversations that implicate parents positively in relation to their children's development of certain skills and knowledges. By tracing the history of a child's knowledge and skills, the relational, social and cultural richness of their life becomes more visible. This provides new options for the child to be on reasonable terms with their own history and provides for the development of a stronger sense of self. (White, 2006a. pp. 127–128)

Postcolonialism

This entry was written by Claire Nettle

Postcolonialism encompasses a range of critical approaches to examining the lasting effects of colonialism in the past and present, from the perspectives of people who have been subject to colonialism and imperialism (Said, 1978; Fanon, 1961). It includes 'subalterns' [those socially, politically, and geographically outside of power structure of the colony and colonial homeland] speaking for themselves about cultural narratives surrounding slavery, colonisation, migration, racialisation, and notions of 'the East' and 'the West' (Spivak, 1993).

'We are challenged to rescue, reconstruct, and define therapeutic metaphors based on our own cultural and historical experiences. This process is what I refer to as the development of a post-colonial therapy.'

Makungu Akinyela

Post-colonial therapy

As colonized people, our healing must come through self-determined action. The task for those of us from African traditions is therefore to take steps in generating and identifying culturally appropriate practices, processes and methods to heal our own. We are challenged to rescue, reconstruct, and define therapeutic metaphors based on our own cultural and historical experiences. This process is what I refer to as the development of a post-colonial therapy. (Akinyela, 2002, p. 32)

It is my hope that a post-colonial therapy could offer a 'liberated territory' in which New Afrikan people could re-value their lives before heading back into a world that is so often hostile to the hopes and dreams of our people. It is also my hope that the development of a post-colonial therapy for New Afrikan people could play a small part in the broader overall struggle to decolonize our minds and spirits. By creating liberated cultural spaces, much the same way that we have created freedom schools, perhaps a genuinely post-colonial therapy can reinvigorate the aspirations of the New Afrikan people, and who knows where this could lead. (Akinyela, 2002, p. 41)

[See POSTCOLONIALISM]

Postcolonial therapy's relationship with poststructuralist therapy

As we are struggling to free ourselves from Euro-centric assumptions and prescriptions for life, it makes sense that there is an overlap with the ways in which some poststructuralist European thinkers and therapists are re-conceptualising the world of therapy. It seems significant to engage with these poststructuralist practices while taking care to define for ourselves the commonalities and the points of departure. Where certain aspects of poststructuralist practice resonate strongly with us, let us ask why this is the case. Are there cultural, historical and social reasons? Which aspects of the poststructuralist approaches fit with our particular cultural project? How are the particular practices of healing linked to our own histories and ongoing practices of culture? How do we wish to engage with these practices in our own ways and our own contexts? (Akinyela, 2002, p. 37)

Poststructuralism (as it relates to narrative practice)

Poststructuralism is a way of thinking that questions the assumptions of structuralism.

Structuralism thinks …	Poststructuralism thinks …	Poststructuralist thought invites us as practitioners to …
The aim of inquiry is to search for 'deep structures' or 'essential truths' about people.	It's important to draw attention to the real effects of the process of looking for 'deep structures' or 'essential truths'. One of these effects in the health professions has been the development of various norms and ideas about what people's lives *should* look like in order to be *healthy*.	Assist people (where relevant) to stop measuring their lives according to what certain social norms say life should be about.
Such a search for 'deep structures' or 'essential truths' can be objective.	What we are looking for, what we believe and where we come from will shape both how we look and what we'll find.	Question therapist 'objectivity', 'expertise' and 'practices of interpretation'.
It is 'deep structure' (eg. inner-self) that shapes life.	Language and the use of language plays a vital role in shaping life. What people say and do and how we relate to each other shapes life. The meanings that we give to the events in our lives, and how we organise these into stories about ourselves and others, shapes life.	Question taken-for-granted ideas and assumptions that might be sustained through the language we are using in therapy. Consider how stories and rituals and other performative aspects are relevant to understanding the process of therapy.
Our ideas, problems, qualities, are linked to some internal self.	Our ideas, problems, qualities are all products of culture and history. They have been created over time and in particular contexts.	Externalise ideas, problems and qualities in therapy conversations.

Poststructuralism (as it relates to narrative practice)

(continued)

Structuralism thinks …	Poststructuralism thinks …	Poststructuralist thought invites us as practitioners to …
Our identities are fixed and essential – to be found within our inner-selves.	Our identities are constantly created in relationship with others, with institutions and with broader relations of power.	Take seriously how every therapy conversation will shape the identity (to some extent) of both the person consulting the therapist and the therapist. Think through how we can involve appreciative witnesses to the work that is occurring in the therapy room. Develop accountability practices to check out the real effects of therapy conversations on those who consult with us.
Our identities are always consistent.	Our identities are made up, and continually being made up, of many (sometimes contradictory) stories.	Consider how the stories of our lives shape our lives and how therapy might enable the rich description of preferred stories of identity.

(This table is from Thomas, 2002, p. 87)

'We also pick daisies, fly kites, eat chocolates, and sponsor dolphins.'

Power to Our Journeys Group

Poststructuralist feminism

During the 1980s and 1990s new ways of engaging with the discourse of feminism became available. Poststructuralist feminism brought a renewed emphasis on the *plurality* of women's experience as opposed to the idea that women as a group are 'unified' with an 'inherent sameness'. Reflecting the broader poststructuralist position, there is scepticism within poststructuralist feminism about the usefulness of conceiving of 'women' as a single group. These feminists challenge the established categories of sex, class, race/ethnicity, and place an emphasis on the multiplicity of meanings in regard to identity. Poststructuralist feminists have stated that there are multiple and particular ways in which all operations of power need to be de-stabilised in each woman's life. Poststructuralist feminism is also interested in unpacking and scrutinising the collection of ideas that have gone into making up feminism so that taken-for-granted notions are rendered visible and attended to, particularly any ways in which universal norms of womanhood have been established which have the effect of both marginalising and reifying difference. (Russell & Carey, 2003, p. 87)

See also Hekman (1996), Weedon (1987), Hare-Mustin & Maracek (1990).

Power to Our Journeys

Power to Our Journeys, a group for people who heard hostile voices (and who had been diagnosed with schizophrenia) was facilitated by Michael White at Dulwich Centre in the late 1980s and early 1990s.

> This is a support group for people who struggle through their lives hearing voices. It is an empowering group enabling our stories and our 'insider' knowledges to be heard and recognised. We have developed close and respectful friendships that help us through the hard times. Each step we take together is about our survival, but these also have to do with justice – because there is so much injustice around issues in the mental health field that needs to be addressed. We also pick daisies, fly kites, eat chocolates, and sponsor dolphins. (Power to Our Journeys in White, 1997, p. 214)

The Power to Our Journeys Group was the first 'hearing voices group' in Australia. It developed at the same time that Patsy Hage and Marius Romme were creating in the Netherlands what was later to become the Hearing Voices Network (see https://www.hearing-voices.org/).

[See INSIDER KNOWLEDGE]

Pride

Aunty Barbara Wingard emphasises the significance of creating contexts for people who are enduring hardship to experience a pride in their knowhow, their skills, and their ancestry:

> Our pride comes from a knowledge of hard times. It is a pride of knowing what we have been through. It is a pride of knowing our stories and finding ways of sharing them with others who want to hear … Pride is a lovely word. It has brought us to where we are today, and it will take us into the future. (Wingard, 2002, p. 152)

Prison abolitionism

Prison abolitionism 'seeks to build an international movement to end the Prison Industrial Complex … by challenging the belief that caging and controlling people makes us safe'. (Critical Resistance, see: http://criticalresistance.org/)

Angela Davis:

> … the prison-industrial complex is a result of the *failure* to enact abolition democracy. 'Abolition democracy' is a term used by DuBois in his work *Black Reconstruction*, his germinal study of the period immediately following slavery. George Lipsitz uses it today within contemporary contexts. I will try to explain briefly its applicability to three forms of abolitionism: the abolition of slavery, the abolition of the death penalty, and the abolition of the prison. DuBois argued that the abolition of slavery was accomplished only in the negative sense. In order to achieve the *comprehensive* abolition of slavery – after the institution was rendered illegal and black people were released from their chains – new institutions should have been created to incorporate black people into the social order … DuBois argues that a host of democratic institutions are needed to fully achieve abolition – thus abolition democracy … In thinking specially about the abolition of prisons using the approach of abolition democracy, we would propose the creation of an array of social institutions that would begin to solve the social problems that set people on the track to prison, thereby helping to render the prison obsolete … Prisons have thrived over the last century, precisely because of the absence of those resources and the persistence of some of the deep structures of slavery. (Davis, 2005, pp. 95–97)

There are rich histories of prison resistance. There are people, both inside and outside, working day and night trying to give voice to the realities of prisons and trying to create alternatives. They are almost exclusively from cultures and communities that have experienced the police and prisons as tools of colonisation … [Their work offers us] invitations … to create new ways of righting wrongs. Invitations to create, with them, new culture and in the process to address the wrongs committed against Indigenous Australians.

Prison abolitionism

(continued)

> I hope that the(ir) voices … challenge and spark the imagination. I believe that they invite us to imagine a 'justice system' based on moving forwards, towards connection, towards restoration of the damage done.
>
> I believe that they invite us to refuse to replicate domination, to instead create places, processes and symbols of hope, and to imagine approaches to crime that, instead of tearing neighbourhoods apart, rebuild relationships and communities.
>
> Through these invitations, the outrage and utter sorrow of prisons can turn instead to dreams of freedom. This country from which I write was invaded to become a prison. We have unique histories. This land knows of prisons like no other. It knows of the sorrow and the violence, and it knows of dreaming. Dreams of freedom lie scattered in the most unexpected of places. It seems time to gather them together. (Denborough, 1995b, p. 14)

Various communities are seeking ways to respond to interpersonal violence without involving police, prisons and the state. For more information see: Creative Interventions: http://www.creative-interventions.org/, Storytelling and Organizing Project: http://www.stopviolenceeveryday.org/, Sisters Inside: https://sistersinside.com.au/, and Gorrie & Church (2018).

[See ABOLITION DEMOCRACY; INCITE! CRITICAL RESISTANCE STATEMENT]

'… the prison-industrial complex is a result of the failure to enact abolition democracy.'

Angela Davis

Privilege

… the word 'privilege' is used in a particular way to describe unearned rights, benefits, immunity, and favours that are bestowed on individuals and groups solely on the basis of their race, culture, religion, gender, sexual orientation, physical ability, or other key characteristic. The use of the word 'privilege' in this way has different histories in different local contexts. Here in Australia, it is a word that feminist women have used to try to articulate the experience of male privilege in a patriarchal culture. Similarly, Indigenous Australians have used the description of white privilege to focus on the discrepancy of experience between white Australians and those subject to racism, dispossession, and colonisation. We encourage you to trace the history of the use of the word in your own context. One of the most significant reasons why we have chosen to use the word 'privilege' in this document is that it places the focus on members of dominant groups (white people, men, heterosexual people, able-bodied people, etc.) and our responsibilities to address relations of power.

It is important to acknowledge that some of us experience privilege in a wide range of domains (e.g. white, professional heterosexual men experience privilege in relation to race, class, gender and sexual orientation), while others may experience privilege in very few, if any, domains of life. Responsibilities for addressing privilege are therefore not equal. (Raheim, et.al, 2004)

[See BECOMING SQUAREHEAD]

Productive power

This entry was written by Claire Nettle

Foucault recognised power as acting not only as a repressive force of constraint, but also as a productive force that can sanction particular 'truths', bring about particular ways of acting, ground particular identities, or even bring them into existence:

> [O]ne of the most innovative aspects of Foucault's theory of power was the insistence on power as a productive and positive force, rather than as a purely negative, repressive entity (McNay, 1992, p. 38).

Unlike coercive force delivered in a single direction from above, productive power operates in diffuse ways, shaping people's knowledge through multiple interactions.

[See DISCOURSE; MODERN POWER; NORMALISATION]

Productive power operates in diffuse ways

Pro-feminist men

On many occasions over the years that I have been presenting this work, others have referred to me as a 'pro-feminist man'. I have always experienced discomfort with this definition of my identity, and have always protested it on several counts. Because men do not have women's experience of the world, I don't believe that men can be pro-feminist by identity. I am for pro-feminist action, but what sort of men's actions are in the interests of women can only be decided upon by women. I am concerned that for men to propose or to accede to a pro-feminist identity is likely to marginalise this consideration – that, under these circumstances, there is a very significant risk that, in judging their actions, men will place faith in their individual consciousness, and cease to actively solicit women's feedback about what is in their interests, and to give this feedback primacy.

I also have difficulty with the notion of a pro-feminist identity because this obscures my own personal stake in any of the actions that I take to challenge men's domination of others. Growing up in men's culture, I have been on the receiving end of men's excesses and abuses of power. And, for a good part of my life, I witnessed, with great heartache, such abuses being inflicted on those whom I love. So, in the actions that I am engaged in to address local injustices, many of which are related to the politics of gender, I am addressing this heartache. It is not just for women that I make it my business to do this – it is for me as well.

… I don't think that it is possible for men to venture very far outside of the dominant men's culture, even if they experience alienation from it, without assistance from women. And, as I have already said, pro-feminist action cannot be a matter of men's individual consciousness. The attention that I give in my work to the politics of gender is an outcome of the conversations that I've had with women who have a feminist politics, and who have been

Pro-feminist men

(continued)

prepared to raise the difficult issues, not so much in regard to the practices of therapy specifically, but in regard to relationships between men and women more generally – women who have been prepared to 'put themselves on the line', in the company of men, in their frank expressions of their experience of these relationships. And, in regard to this, and much, much more, I would particularly like to acknowledge the conversations that Cheryl White and I have shared through the history of our connection. These have been conversations in the context of a partnership in which Cheryl has constantly questioned the limits on what I have been able to think in regard to gender, and, for that matter, culture and race. I have experienced this partnership as a fount of generativity. (White, 1995e, pp. 8–9)

This piece was written more than twenty years ago. If it was written now, it would be written differently, shaped by trans and non-binary experiences, activism, writings and politics.

'I don't think that it is possible for men to venture very far outside of the dominant men's culture, even if they experience alienation from it, without assistance from women.'

Michael White

Pronouns

Pronouns are like shortcuts and we use them a lot when referring to other people. They are a part of many languages. Some of the most common English personal pronouns are: he/him/his; she/her/hers; they/them/theirs. We often use these terms without thinking to stand in for a person's name. Some pronouns in English are gendered. For instance, he/him/his and she/her/hers.

These pronouns are connected to broader ideas about gender. 'He' and 'him' have been loaded with implications, as have 'she' and 'her' – so much so that if I tell you a story about a 'him' or a 'her' and give no other identifying information, your mind might start to make all sorts of assumptions about that person and how they look or act in the world.

Many other words in English are also gendered: man, woman, boy and girl are obvious ones, but there are others like mother, father, daughter, son, aunt, uncle, husband, wife, niece and nephew. Many of these words have alternatives that describe the same thing without implying gender, for example person, child, parent or partner. Have you heard the word 'nibling' in place of niece or nephew? Isn't it the cutest word?

There is nothing essentially problematic about gendered language or any of these words. However, they shape how we interact with people and they shape our identities. Gendered pronouns and gendered language (in many cultures) are linked to the idea that there are two genders, male and female, and that these are distinct, discrete and opposite. This male–female gender binary has massive implications for our lives (that may be the understatement of the century) …

Pronouns
(continued)

> Some people change the pronouns that they use through the course of their lives. This is in part because none of us gets to choose our first pronouns – they are allocated to us at birth. Some people are referred to as she/her in the first part of their lives, and later get referred to as he/him. Some people use he/him as kids, then later use she/her. Others use both or either depending on the circumstances, or use a non-gendered pronoun like they/their …
>
> You might not be able to guess which pronouns fit for some people who are trans or gender nonconforming. When someone is referred to by the wrong pronouns or with other inappropriately gendered terms, this is called 'misgendering'. When this is done intentionally, it is disrespectful and an act of violence (on a continuum of violence that trans and gender-nonconforming people face) …
>
> Misgendering (even when not intentional) can have harmful effects. Spaces where misgendering occurs a lot might simply become inaccessible. When people in our community cannot access spaces or services (such as workplaces, schools, communities or doctors) without experiencing harm, this can have serious and material consequences for people's wellbeing. (Maeder & Dulwich Centre, 2018)

For ideas and stories about ways of avoiding misgendering others, see: www.dulwichcentre.com.au/misgendering

Psychological needs

How many of you have psychological needs? Just raise your hand if you have psychological needs. I'm not asking you to confess these, okay. Although that could be very interesting. But I just would like to know whether you have them or not. I can see many people agreeing. I'm not surprised because, in western culture, people have had psychological needs since 1929. They've been around since 1929. And they're increasingly popular, today more and more people have psychological needs. So, this was a new understanding. Action as a surface manifestation of a psychological need, is a relatively new idea, in the history of the world's culture. It's a novel idea. (Michael White, 2018)

Publishing

Feminist critique of conventional professional publishing processes led Cheryl White and Amanda Kamsler, in 1990, to circulate 'An open invitation to formulate policies around publishing':

> We believe questions are being asked about the way writers have represented the experience of people whose lives and stories they are describing. Where people's actions are under discussion in the literature without their permission – no matter who they are and what is being said – these people are at the mercy of the writer's descriptions about their behaviour … As a result of these considerations, there is now a greater importance being placed on the accurate representation of people's experience in articles and presentations. A number of Australian and New Zealand papers are now being co-authored by the therapist and the persons with whom they met in therapy. There has been a move away from the practice of writers discussing clinical examples as if their own perspective was the 'correct' one. There has been a greater respect for the perspectives of family members in descriptions of the process of therapy ... (quoted in White, 2016, p. 55)

Dulwich Centre Publications continues to grapple with the complexities of the politics of representation in publishing: https://dulwichcentre.com.au/submission-information/

q

p

Queer

A term used to describe a range of sexual orientations and gender identities. Although once used as a derogatory term, the term queer now encapsulates political ideas of resistance to heteronormativity and homonormativity and is often used as an umbrella term to describe the full range of LGBTIQ+ identities. (Child Family Community Australia, 2017).

[See QUEER ACTIVISM; QUEER THEORY]

Queer activism

Queer activism builds on the revolutionary action of Marsha P. Johnson, Sylvia Rivera and others at the Stonewall Inn riot and later in ACTUP – the AIDS Coalition to Unleash Power (See King, 2015):

> Queer activism challenged previous identity-politics gay activism, which regarded sexuality as an essential, inherent component of the self. Activists emphasized militant protest against, rather than assimilation into, current systems, often through visible and confrontational tactics, such as taking over public spaces or outing closeted public figures. They were making the point that public space was heterosexual space and that alternatives to dominant culture were required by queers. Further examples of queer activism include: Queeruption (part of the queercore offshoot of punk): an anarchist movement opposed to the lack of diversity in mainstream gay culture and its embrace of consumerism. Gay shame: a radical alternative to the commercialisation of mainstream Gay Prides with their corporate sponsorship, ticketed events, and celebrity focus. (Barker & Scheele, 2016, p. 54)

Queer theory

Queer theory rejects biological theories of sexual identity and calls into question so-called 'natural' sexuality. Central to these ideas is the challenge to the gender binary system that produces and maintains binary constructions such as male/female and hetero/homo.

Queer theory asks questions such as: Who do these categories serve? Who do these categories include and whom do they exclude? Who has the power to define the categories? How are the categories policed? How do these categories change over time and across cultures? (Tilsen & Nylund, 2010, p. 66) r

Rape culture

A society or environment whose prevailing social attitudes have the effect of normalizing or trivialising sexual assault and abuse.

Re-authoring conversations

[In] … re-authoring conversations, people are invited to attach significance to … previously neglected events, and they are encouraged to link these together with other events of their lives in sequences that unfold through time according to alternative themes, or to what can be referred to as the 'counter-plots' of their lives. As well, in this process, as people are invited … to reflect on the events of these alternative themes or counter-plots, there is new opportunity for them to form identity descriptions that contradict the negative identity conclusions that are associated with what have been the more dominant stories of their lives. (White, 2011c, p. 6)

Reclaiming our stories, reclaiming our lives

The first narrative community gathering which involved Aboriginal families from across South Australia who had lost a loved one due to a death in custody (police stations, prisons) was called 'Reclaiming our stories, reclaiming our lives'. (See Aboriginal Health Council of South Australia, 1995).

[See COMMUNITY GATHERINGS]

Redstockings manifesto

A frequently quoted document from Redstockings of New York, a feminist group, which includes the following: … 'Because we [women] have lived so intimately with our oppressors, in isolation from each other, we have been kept from seeing our personal suffering as a political condition. This creates the illusion that a woman's relationship with her man is a matter of interplay between two unique personalities, and can be worked out individually. In reality, every such relationship is a class relationship, and the conflicts between individual men and women are political conflicts that can only be solved collectively. We regard our personal experience, and our feelings about that experience, as the basis for an analysis of our common situation.' (Redstockings, 1970, quoted in Kramarae, & Treichler, 1985, p. 164)

Refusal of individuality linked to the economy

The political, ethical, social, philosophical problem of our day is not to try to liberate the individual from the economy … but to liberate us both from the economy and from the type of individualization that is linked to the economy. We have to promote new forms of subjectivity through the refusal of this kind of individuality which has been imposed on us for several centuries. (Foucault, 1983, p. 216)

[See NEOLIBERALISM]

'… conflicts between individual men and women are political conflicts that can only be solved collectively …'

Redstocking Manifesto

Relationship anarchy

Relationship anarchy (RA), and relationshipqueer, are words for relationship styles, which question the idea that romantic relationships should be privileged over other kinds of relationships – both culturally and in individuals' lives. Of course many people have relationships that are as close and/or valued as romantic relationships, e.g. relationships with family, friends, colleagues or work partners, companion animals, etc. However, they may struggle to find ways for these relationships to be recognised by others, and by wider society. RA and queer platonic relationships explicitly challenge the hierarchical view of relationships and commitments. (Barker, 2018, pp. 51–52)

Relationship anarchy also seeks to question relationship hierarchies within many forms of polyamory. RA like all forms of anarchism opposes hierarchy. (Mary Heath, personal communication, 21st February 2019)

[See POLYAMORY; OPEN NON-MONOGAMIES]

Relationship dynamics

How many of you have relationship dynamics? Raise your hand if you have relationship dynamics? I'm not surprised … because these have been around since the 1960s. A lot of people have relationship dynamics these days. In fact, they're becoming increasingly popular. Relationship dynamics have been very successful … I'm not saying that before the onset of relationship dynamics … that people were happier in their relationships with others. At times they were still miserable, and in conflict. It wasn't constructed in terms of dynamics, is that clear? That's a new construction. (Michael White, 2018)

Relations of power (hearing voices)

> The experience of hearing voices is all about power, but I never tell people to try to get rid of the voices. If someone is being tyrannised by a particular voice then it is the experience of tyranny that needs addressing. Over the last fifteen years, it has been recognised that sexual abuse and physical abuse are all about power. If you're sexually abused, you're offered counselling. If you're physically abused, you're offered counselling. But if you're verbally abused by voices you are given medication and there is rarely any consideration given to relations of power. So often, the voices that people hear are the voices of those who have physically or sexually abused them. These matters need addressing. Ways must be found for people to reclaim control over their own lives. (Bullimore, 2003, p. 24)

Relinquishing professional position

Mickey de Valda, from the Hearing Voices Network, explains the political significance of professionals relinquishing their position:

> These days more professional people are interested in being involved in hearing voices groups. This is a good thing. It means our work is becoming increasingly respected and acknowledged. There is no doubt in my mind that professionals have skills that enable them to work in a perceptive and sympathetic fashion. The fact that they do not themselves hear voices must however be noted. Wherever possible, the groups need to be facilitated by voice-hearers. If a professional person starts up a group, to get it going, then it is often possible to identify a voice-hearer or two who, with training and support, could take over this facilitation. Once these voice-hearers begin to emerge from the group, the professional facilitators can support them, try to find them access to that training, etc. We are just ordinary people and we may never have run groups before, so we need the training just as others do. But if professionals are willing to stand out of the road, to take a back seat, to relinquish their professional position and to support us, then this is a way to give voice-hearers space to create the groups that are most meaningful to us. We often cannot do this alone. It requires partnership. (de Valda, 2003, p. 17)

Re-membering

Barbara Myerhoff (1982) described identity as an association or a club. Michael White engaged with this metaphor to develop re-membering conversations:

> The membership of this association of life is made up of the significant figures of a person's history, as well as the identities of the person's present circumstances, whose voices are influential with regard to how the person constructs his or her own identity. Re-membering conversations provide an opportunity for people to engage in a revision of the membership of their associations of life, affording an opening for the reconstruction of their identity … In the therapeutic context, re-membering conversations … contribute to the development of a multi-voiced sense of identity, rather than the single-voiced sense of identity that is a feature of the encapsulated self … This is a sense of identity that features positive but non-heroic conclusions about one's actions in life and about who one is. (White, 2007, pp. 136–138)

When people's identities have been shaped by figures who have been abusive and/or oppressive, re-membering conversations are about redistributing storytelling rights.

[See STORYTELLING RIGHTS]

Representing a social issue

A key aspect of collective narrative practice involves acknowledging that people represent not only themselves when they share stories of hardship/injustice but also social issues. This recognition opens different possibilities for action:

> - To conceive of the person meeting with us as representing a social issue.
> - To enable the person to join a collective endeavour in addressing, in some local way, this social issue.
> - To enable people to speak through us, not just to us. (Denborough, 2008, p. 16)

[See COLLECTIVE NARRATIVE PRACTICE; ENABLING CONTRIBUTION; SPEAKING THROUGH US NOT JUST TO US]

Resurrecting diversity in everyday life

[See EXOTICISING THE DOMESTIC]

Returning the gaze

I'll float one example here, one that relates to the idea of returning the 'gaze', or turning the gaze back on itself. For those people who are the recipients of ward rounds, for them to research these ward rounds can be very empowering. This might engage them in a study of who can speak, under what circumstances they can speak, which ways of speaking are acknowledged, which ways of speaking are disqualified, whose authority is privileged, the effects of the privileging of this voice, and so on. I find that many people are quite taken by the introduction of this idea, and that it has a positive effect even if it is not taken up in any formalised way. (White, 1995b, p. 122)

'For those people who are the recipients of ward rounds, for them to research these ward rounds can be very empowering.'

Michael White

Riverbank position

David Denborough: I have heard you describe the importance of enabling children to have a 'different place to stand' prior to speaking about the trauma that they may have experienced. Can you say more about this?

Michael White: Developing the second story is like developing a different territory of identity in which a child can stand and look out at their life, and reflect upon what they have been through. Once this different territory of life has been developed or redeveloped it becomes safe for a child to speak about the trauma they have been through.

I was recently teaching in Zimbabwe with a group of workers who respond to children who have been affected by HIV/AIDS. Within this group a metaphor was offered [by Caleb Wakhungu] that beautifully describes this process. This metaphor was of assisting people to 'stand on the riverbank' in order to look at the river of life. According to the way this metaphor was employed, if one is floundering in the actual river in which the story of trauma dominates, and one is left struggling with the currents that are flowing past and around them, it is not possible to think differently about the events in which one has been immersed. But if one is standing in a different territory of identity, a territory that gives one a riverbank on which to stand, it is possible to look over the events of one's life, to re-visit them, to speak about them and to think differently about them, without being re-traumatised, without being swept along by the current …

David Denborough: The metaphor of a riverbank is a beautiful one … it's not implying that the trauma story isn't significant, just that a child needs a different place to stand in relation to it …

Riverbank position

(continued)

Michael White: Yes. This second story provides a different territory of identity, like a riverbank, on which the child can stand when giving expression to their experiences of trauma. Standing on the riverbank makes it possible to look back and give voice to stories of trauma without being defined by the trauma. When standing on the riverbank it becomes possible to express experiences of trauma in ways that feature themes of outrage and reflections on injustice rather than as failure and shame. It is often the case that it only becomes possible for children, or for adults for that matter, to give a full account of what they have been through after they have another territory on which to stand. The second story provides a foundation for people to then give expression to experiences of trauma in ways that are healing and not retraumatising. Furthermore, once the second story becomes richly described, it becomes a driving force for further healing actions. It becomes a driving force for people to take next steps that are in harmony with the understandings of what they give value to, and with what they intend for their lives, which are represented in this second story. (White, 2006b, pp. 88–90)

[See SECOND STORY]

S

Safe territory of identity

[See RIVERBANK POSITION]

Saying hullo again

Saying hullo again questions open up the possibility for people experiencing grief to reclaim their relationship with the lost loved one:

- If you were seeing yourself through Ron's eyes right now, what would you be noticing about yourself that you could appreciate?
- What difference would it make to how you feel if you were appreciating this in yourself right now?
- What do you know about yourself that you are awakened to when you bring alive the enjoyable things that Ron knew about you?
- What difference would it make to you if you kept this realisation, about yourself, alive on a day-to-day basis?
- What difference would feeling this way make to the steps that you could take to get back into life? (White, 1988a, p. 20)

In focussing here on the 'saying hullo' metaphor, I am not taking a position against the utilisation of the saying goodbye metaphor. There is much to say goodbye to, including to a material reality and to hopes and expectations, etc. Instead, I believe that the process of grief is a 'saying goodbye and then saying hullo' phenomenon.

Having said this, I would argue that every experience of loss is unique, as are the requirements for the resolution of every loss. Any metaphor is only helpful to the extent that it recognises, and facilitates the expression of, this uniqueness, and doesn't subject persons to normative specifications. (White, 1988a, p. 28)

Second story

When meeting with children about experiences of trauma, the story of this trauma and the effects that this has had on the child's life is often the first story that is brought to our attention. This story requires recognition.

But there is also a second story of how the child has responded to these experiences of trauma, and this second story is often overlooked. No-one is a passive recipient of trauma. Even children respond in ways to lessen the effects of the trauma, to seek comfort, to try to preserve what is precious to them, and so on. This second story is very important. The ways in which children respond to trauma are based on certain skills. These skills reflect what the child gives value to. And what the child gives value to is linked to the child's history, to their family, to their community, and to their culture.

These responses to trauma are not solely individual. They are not formed independently of the contribution of others. In these responses, children are linked to key figures of their lives. In narrative practice we are very interested in developing rich accounts of this second story. By developing rich accounts of this second story we reconnect children to culture, to family, to community, and to history. (White, 2006b, pp. 87–88)

[See SUBORDINATE STORYLINE; REAUTHORING]

Self-narrative

In striving to make sense of our lives, we face the task of arranging our experiences of events in sequences across time in such a way as to arrive at a coherent account of ourselves. Specific experiences of events of the past and the present, and those that are predicted to occur in the future, are connected to develop this account, which has been referred to as a story or self-narrative. (White, 1988a, p. 22)

'Even children respond in ways to lessen the effects of the trauma, to seek comfort, to try to preserve what is precious to them, and so on.'

Michael White

Senior men's moods

We all have experiences of the dominant men's culture, and many aspects of this experience are profoundly negative. My guess is that most of the readers of this transcript could readily relate stories about circumstances of their lives under which what they've said and how they have acted has been considerably determined by the moods of some senior male. And a very great number of us have been taught to fear and to be beware of these moods. So, when confronted by the moods of senior men, we are somewhat vulnerable to stepping into behaviour that goes against our own better judgment, that compromises our chosen values, that violates our relationships with our 'selves'. So, it makes a great deal of sense for us to take responsibility for the monitoring of our responses to the senior men in therapeutic contexts. This affords some chance of determining whether or not our perceptions of the man's mood are determining of our responses in this work. Needless to say, if these moods are determining of our responses' to the other members of the families that consult us, then we are undoubtedly contributing to their experience of oppression. (White, 1995c, p. 109)

Shared textual heritage

Generating shared textual heritage across generations is one approach within collective narrative practice to seek to address conflict between generations:

> Time and again, members of the older generation witnessed young people speaking about treasured values and dreams, and linking these to histories which were resonant to the older generations. The reverse was also true. As the older generations traced the histories of their values, skills, and hopes, this intrigued and delighted those who were younger. And so the older generations honoured the younger generation's histories, and vice-versa. In the process, a shared 'textual heritage' (Werstch, 2002) evolved.
>
> We were not interested in creating a nostalgic, romantic or single-storied version of history or heritage in this process. What makes rich textual heritage is not conformity, but diversity. Throughout this process, as the generations shared the social histories of what they valued, we were not seeking to compromise history (to imply that the older and younger generations share the same history) but instead to make it possible for the different generations to consider and respect each other's histories. We could understand this as taking, in Barenboim's terms, an 'artistic' approach to conflict and to history (Barenboim & Said, 2004, p. 60). Starting in the present, with people's current diverse skills, hopes and values, and then linking these to social histories, creates richly-textured multiple-storied histories. In doing so, it provides the generations with different ways of relating to each other's past and present.
>
> This process was also engaging in what Paulo Freire (1994) describes as 'the invention of unity in diversity' (p. 157) … the values, skills, hopes, and histories that the community members described [were all vibrantly different]. Diversity was apparent and celebrated, and yet a sense of unity or harmony was also performed due to the mutual honouring of histories. Harmony seems a particularly appropriate metaphor. We are aiming to bring the storylines of the different generations into harmonic relationship. Within the musical realm, harmony is created when different musical lines are in resonant relationship with each other. Like the storylines between generations, these musical lines are different and yet, with care, can be played in harmony. (Denborough, 2010a, p. 9)

Silencing

Power to Our Journeys:

> Over the many years of our different connections with psychiatric services, we have found little opportunity to speak openly of our day-to-day experiences of the voices and visions that have been so troublesome to us, or, for that matter, the voices and visions that have been helpful to our lives. We have been silenced time and again by many psychiatric professionals who have consistently refused to acknowledge our experiences of these voices and visions. At times we have been bewildered by this, at a loss to understand it. At times we have linked this silencing to the fear we see in the eyes of others. Perhaps they experience this fear because we put them in touch with how vulnerable they might be in their own struggles in life, and with a realisation of how thin the line is between where they stand in life and where we stand in life. At other times we understand others believe that to make space for us to talk more openly about our experiences of troublesome voices and visions is counterproductive. We know that still others are caught up in weird theories about our experiences, and talk about our lives in ways that subtract from our sense of self-respect and make it impossible for them to hear what we have to say about our experiences of voices and visions. And we meet others who are so caught up in professional career and institutional considerations of a hierarchical nature that it is impossible for them to be with us in healing ways.
>
> Needless to say, this silencing has profoundly negative consequences for all of our lives. All of us have felt abandoned because of this. We have not felt joined with by others at those times in our lives when this was what we have longed for most. At times this very silencing has contributed to a sense that we might be going mad. And it has made it virtually impossible for us to change our relationship with the troublesome voices and visions that have been so dominating of our lives, and, as well, with the voices and visions that have been more supportive of us. (Brigitte, Sue, Mem & Veronika, 1997, pp. 205–6)

[See POWER TO OUR JOURNEYS]

Sistergirl / Brotherboy

Terms used for transgender people within some Aboriginal or Torres Strait Islander communities. Sistergirls and Brotherboys have distinct cultural identities and roles. Sistergirls are Indigenous women who were classified male at birth but live their lives as women, including taking on traditional cultural female practices. Brotherboys are Indigenous transgender people, whose bodies were considered female at birth but 'choose to live their lives as male, regardless of which stage/path medically they choose' (Child Family Community Australia, 2017).

For more information see Sisters & Brothers NT: https://www.facebook.com/SistersBrothersNTCelebratingDiversity/

[See TWO SPIRIT]

Smash that discourse!

During one of the teaching blocks of the Master of Narrative Therapy and Community Work, Aunty Shirley Simpson spoke passionately of how she is defying the implication that as an Aboriginal woman she will die at a young age. Aunty Shirley's rallying cry of 'Smash that discourse!' had such resonance that t-shirts were made bearing her words, see: https://vimeo.com/310226129

Social action / social 'movement'

If we wish to ensure that, at the very least, our ways of working are not diminishing the possibilities for collective local actions, then it may be necessary for us to develop a framework by which to reflect on the effects of our work. There is a rich tradition of critique in relation to how therapeutic discourse can 'personalise' and 'individualise' social and political issues (Kitzinger & Perkins, 1993; Prilleltensky, 1994). These are critiques that I believe are worth taking seriously and responding to. I don't believe there is any need for us to be defensive about this. Instead, we can engage with the critique and develop ways of continually reflecting upon whether our work is creating conditions in which local social action / social movement is more or less likely. The following 'checklist' is one that I find helpful in reflecting upon my own work.

- Are the people I am working with experiencing an increased sense of agency?
- Are they becoming more knowledgeable about their own skills, knowledges, abilities, that can be put to use in addressing the difficulties that they (and others) are facing? Are they experiencing putting these into action and seeing the results in their own lives?
- Is our work linking people together around shared concerns and also around their skills, knowledges, and abilities?
- Are the people we are working with being enabled to experience making a contribution to the lives of others?

Social action / social 'movement'
(continued)

- Are the broader social, historical, cultural factors that are influencing the strength of the problem they are facing becoming articulated and named? If so, is this generating dissatisfaction with the status quo?
- Are the people we are working with becoming linked with stories, histories and knowledge about how local initiatives, skills and knowledge can bring about changes? In other words, are they experiencing increasing hope in contrast to fatalism?
- Are there ways in which those with whom we are working are becoming actively engaged in the creation of collective folk culture (music, art, drama, literature) around themes of addressing the difficulties, injustices, being faced by themselves and others?
- Are there ways in which they are experiencing acknowledgement and celebration of these expressions of local culture?
- To what degree is our work a collective endeavour, involving partnership and collaboration with other colleagues?
- Are we taking care to ensure that metaphors of healing are not precluding metaphors of local action?
- Are we inviting rigorous critique and questioning of our work – about ways in which we may be inadvertently replicating the status quo, or normative ideas in relation to gender, class, race, sexual identity, and so on?
- To what degree is our work inviting people to re-engage with personal/social history, and to what degree is it inviting a rearrangement of the current social world? (Denborough, 2008, pp. 194–5)

Solidarity

> And what of solidarity? I am thinking of a solidarity that is constructed by therapists who refuse to draw a sharp distinction between their lives and the lives of others, who refuse to marginalize those persons who seek help; by therapists who are prepared to constantly confront the fact that if faced with circumstances such that provide the context of the troubles of others, they just might not be doing nearly as well themselves. (White, 1993, p. 132)

'Solidarity' is the title of one of the most influential Power to Our Journeys documents:

> This document is a declaration of solidarity. It is a declaration of the fact that the members of the Power to Our Journeys group are uniting and standing together against the forces that have attempted to tyrannise our lives. This is a way of giving notice to the voices, which, try as they might, will not, in the end, succeed in their attempts to capture our lives. We will carry with us the spirit of this group as we walk through life, and at those times when we are stretched and most vulnerable to being hassled by the voices, we will recreate the experience of this solidarity. This will provide for us a great deal of security and comfort in the face of adversity. (Brigitte, Sue, Mem & Veronika, 1997, p. 213)

Speak through us not just to us

> … there are many instances in which it is simply not culturally appropriate to ask someone direct questions about their personal experience or history. For instance, when meeting with young men in remote Indigenous Australian communities … it would make no sense for these young men to start to talk to me about their personal experiences of life, let alone any difficulties they may be facing. Why would they talk to a stranger about these things? But if I ask the young men if they wish to send a story through me of how they are dealing with difficult times to other young men in different communities who are grappling with the same issues that they are facing, this is a different matter entirely. This makes sense: it makes it possible to speak about many things, even very difficult things, because there is a collective purpose involved. The conversation is not then focusing on their 'individual experience' and it is not directed to me. Instead, the conversation is focusing on what contribution they can make to others and it just happens to be directed through me (or other practitioners). (Denborough, 2008, p. 16)

Spirituality

The Just Therapy Team at the Family Centre in Aotearoa, New Zealand, have grappled to develop a contemporary and inclusive spirituality:

> Spirituality posed a considerable problem for us at The Family Centre. We had formed a cultural partnership of Maori, Pacific Island and Pakeha (European) workers and developed an agency that was determined to honour the cultures, address our colonial history and develop new expressions of equity. Spirituality posed a major problem for us, because in the European world it is largely viewed as a personal matter that has no role in the work place. Whereas for our Maori and Samoan colleagues it was inconceivable to consider health and wellbeing as ever being disconnected from overt expressions of spirituality …
>
> Spirituality to us is essentially about *relationship*. For us relationship is expressed in four primary ways. The first of these is the primary relationship between *people and the environment*. By this we refer to the land, the mountains, the sea, the sky and so on. Anything that promotes or facilitates the relationship between people and the environment, to us, is spiritual … The second relationship we understand to be spiritual is that between *people*

Spirituality
(continued)

and other people in terms of justice and love. Whenever people are practising justice and love, whether it is in a household, in a community, in a nation, or internationally, it is spiritual to us. Any act of kindness, any act of love, any act of beauty, is an act of the sacred. We talk about justice and love because justice without love can be harsh, and love without justice can be sloppy and even unjust …

The third relationship we focus on is that between *people and their heritage*, their ancestry, their forefathers and mothers, those who have gone before. That which honours people's heritage is spiritual in our view …

The final relationship we speak about concerning spirituality is between *people and the numinous.* We cannot find a better English word than numinous for that which is other, beyond, transcendent, or what some people call God. For us, that which affirms connections beyond the physical seeing, touching, measurable environment to the numinous is spiritual. That which works against this and defines the material, measurable world as the sum total of significant life, is to us, the antithesis of spirituality.

With this understanding of spirituality, we have been able to both share together and feel comfortable despite our very different cultural heritages … (Waldegrave, 2000, pp. 162–165).

'Any act of kindness, any act of love, any act of beauty, is an act of the sacred.'

Charles Waldegrave

Spiritualities – ascendant and immanent

Ascendant forms of spirituality are achieved on planes that are imagined at an altitude above everyday life. It is when people succeed in rising to these altitudes that they experience God's blessing, whomever that God might be. It is on these planes that an understanding of what would approximate a direct correspondence between God's word and one's life is attainable; it is on this plane that it becomes possible to achieve a relatively unmediated expression of God's word.

Immanent forms of spirituality are achieved not by locating oneself at some altitude above one's life, but by descending into the caverns that are imagined deep below the surface of one's life. This is a spirituality that is achieved by 'being truly and wholly who one really is', 'by being in touch with one's true nature', by being faithful to the god of self. Much of popular psychology is premised on a version of this notion of an immanent spirituality – to worship a self through being at one with one's 'nature'.

And then there are *immanent/ascendant forms* of spirituality, in which spirituality is achieved by being in touch with or having an experience of a soul or the divine that is deep within oneself and that is manifest through one's relationship with a god who is ascendant. (White, 2000c, pp. 131–132)

[See SPIRITUALITIES OF THE SURFACE]

Spiritualities of the surface

Although I find many of the contemporary immanent/ascendant notions of spirituality to be quite beautiful, and the notion of the soul far more aesthetically pleasing than the notion of the psyche, and although I remain interested in exploring the proposals for life or, if you like, the ethics, that are associated with these notions of spirituality, I am more interested in what might be called the material versions of spirituality. Perhaps we could call these the spiritualities of the surface.

The spiritualities of the surface have to do with material existence. These are the spiritualities that can be read in the shape of people's identity projects, in the steps that people take in the knowing formation of the self. This is a form of spirituality that concerns one's personal ethics, that concerns the modes of being and thought that one enters one's life into, that is reflected in the care that one takes to attain success in a style of living. This is a transformative spirituality in that it so often has to do with becoming other than the received version of who one is. This is a form of spirituality that relates not to the nonmaterial, but to the tangible. And I believe that this is the sort of spirituality to which Foucault referred in his work on the ethics of the self (1988a, 1988b). (White, 2000c, p. 132)

[See SPIRITUALITIES – ASCENDANT AND IMMAMENT]

Sponsoring diversity not conformity

[See EXOTICISING THE DOMESTIC]

Storyline of identity

> Who we are and what we do are influenced by the stories that we tell about ourselves. While we can't always change the stories that others have about us, we can influence the stories we tell about ourselves and those we care about. And we can, with care, rework or rewrite storylines of identity … This is what we do in life. We take certain events and then link them together into a plot or theme. And this plot or theme about our lives then shapes our identities – who we are. (Denborough, 2014, pp. 3–4)

[See SELF-NARRATIVE]

Storytelling rights

Stephen Madigan:

> The idea of storytelling rights and the question of 'who has the story telling rights to the story being told' has been a jump off point of understanding and meaning making in my learning and training. In 1993 I expanded the idea of storytelling rights to include a narrative questioning practice in line with the charter of human rights and justice from the UN within the eating disorder hospital ward I was consulting to. Therapeutic letter writing campaigns (based on the practice of writing to governments during my life in the anti-nuclear movement etc.) emerged as a practice and the hospital ward adopted our charter of Anti-anorexia rights and freedoms. We further performed the idea by financially hiring peer/insiders as 'persons with knowledge' to teach in our Vancouver School of Narrative Therapy training program in 1994. It was a lovely and dramatic period of politic and practice exploration.

[See CHARTER (DRAFT) OF STORYTELLING RIGHTS]

Strong stories

A term/concept used by Aboriginal narrative practitioner Tileah Drahm-Butler (2015) to represent the stories that tell of the ways that a person or people have stood up to problems in their lives.

> When people present for counselling, a problem story has often convinced them of negative ideas about their identity. This problem story might be influenced by ideas of Western normality that lead our people to feel bad about themselves. Behind this problem story though, is an alternative story, a strong story. This *strong* story tells of the ways that a person has stood up to the problem. Narrative practice is interested in what's called double-story development – finding ways to reduce the power of the problem story and to draw out and reinforce the strong story. This is true for individuals and also for Aboriginal people more generally.
>
> Within our *collective* story is the experience of ongoing colonisation. The very systems that govern our lives are built on colonial ideals which compete against Indigenous World Views and through which racism is perpetrated and perpetuated (Rigney, 1999). There is a collective experience of this injustice and racism which has led to common experiences of hardship and makes our personal experience political. There is, however, also a collective and common experience of resistance and resilience for Aboriginal peoples across Australia. These stories are traced throughout our history and continue today. We often share these stories of resilience and survival within our families as they serve as a source of strength … Wherever there are stories of hardship, there are also stories of resistance to this hardship that continue to sustain us and link us to the stories of our ancestors. (Drahm-Butler, 2015, pp. 26–27)

Subordinate storyline (also known as alternative story)

I will refer to 'subordinate storyline' development when describing the further development of some of the alternative stories of children's lives that are to be found in thin traces, in the shadows of the dominant stories of their lives. This description seems apt, as it is not by chance that these storylines are relatively invisible at the outset of therapeutic conversations. These storylines have been subordinated in the context of the politics of disqualification, diminishment, ridicule and marginalisation. (White, 2006c, p. 165)

Successful therapy

Donald: What would be the criteria of successful therapy from your perspective?

Michael: I'm really interested in what persons determine to be preferred ways of living and interacting with themselves and each other. That's one of my major interests in this work. If the ways of living and thinking that persons often come into therapy with aren't working for them, for whatever reason, I'm interested in providing a context that contributes to the exploration of other ways of living and thinking. There is always a stock of alternative stories about how life might be, other versions of life as lived. I'm interested in how I might assist persons to step more into those stories that are judged, by them, to be preferred – to perform the alternative understandings or meanings that these alternative stories make possible. Of course, this is not unproblematic, and there are many institutions in our society that stand in the way of this. And at times this means joining with persons in the challenging of certain structures that make this domination possible. So, at times, this practice of therapy includes a form of political action at what we might call the local level. (White, 1995d, pp. 19–20)

'I am interested in how narrative practices can be used to connect individual stories to collective stories to sustain us through problem times.'

Tileah Drahm-Butler

Survivance

In her forms of Aboriginal narrative practice, Tileah Drahm-Butler (2015) draws upon the concept of survivance:

> Vizenor (1991) uses the term *Survivance* to discuss this, a term that includes *Survival and Resistance*, representing that Aboriginal people, and Indigenous people around the world, have retained spirituality and culture in resistance to colonisation. I am interested in how narrative practices can be used to connect individual stories to collective stories to sustain us through problem times. (Drahm-Butler, 2015, p. 27)

[See YARNING AS SPIRITUAL PRACTICE]

t

J

Taking-it-back practices

Taking-it-back practices involve therapists embracing an ethical responsibility to identify the ways in which therapeutic conversations are shaping of their work and lives, and in which they acknowledge the contributions of the persons who consult them to this. (See White, 1997, pp. 132–146)

Team of Life narrative approach

A way of working originally developed to respond to former child soldiers whose love of football (soccer) invited/challenged David Denborough (2008) to create a form of narrative practice using a sporting metaphor that did not require young people to speak in the first person about their lives.

The medium and the message

One of the dimensions of critical thinking described by Mary Heath (2012):

> It is likely that in any communication, there will be both overt and implicit messages, even if the person making the communication is not consciously intending to communicate the implicit messages, which may seem so natural and normal to him or her that they pass unnoticed. It is useful therefore to ask what the overt message/s and implicit message/s are. We can then ask how the medium chosen invites us to accept the overt message/s and the implicit message/s. Is the medium inviting an emotional response that renders us more likely to accept these messages? Sometimes I find myself watching a film or TV show where the music and images are inviting me to sympathise with someone or some actions that I would usually find objectionable. Having realised this, I can make choices about whether this is a valuable opportunity to reconsider my previous position, or whether I might resist the pull of emotion raised by the music and images since it conflicts with an ethical position I am strongly attached to for good reasons. I might decide that my previous position, while basically correct, lacked compassion. (Heath, 2012, p. 17)

The person is not the problem, the problem is the problem

A phrase that has come to be synonymous with narrative therapy and represents its non-pathologizing ethic:

> … the idea of 'the person is not the problem, the problem is the problem' … was a key development, because most models of the time (whether individual psychotherapy or family therapy) involved various ways of making the person the problem. Most of the individual psychotherapy of the time understood the client as the problem, as if they were causing or even in some way 'wanted' the problem. In the systemic family therapy models of the time, the problem was routinely blamed on the family or the family system. Yes, the idea and practice of not blaming the people but saying 'the problem is the problem' was a radical notion that set narrative approaches in contrast to other prevailing therapy models. (Findlay, 2016, p. 20)

[See EXTERNALISING]

The person is not the problem, the problem is the problem, and the solution is not only personal

> Collective narrative practice is based on externalising principles and on taking them one step further. It becomes possible to externalise the problems people are facing *and* enable possibilities for collective contributions. In this way, 'The person is not the problem, the problem is the problem and … the solution is not only personal'. I am interested in ensuring that, once the problem is externalised (therefore placed in the social realm), the solution does not simply return to a personal one, and that, instead, opportunities are created for collective contribution; opportunities are created for people to contribute to 'social movement'. (Denborough, 2008, p. 192)

[See EXTERNALISING; SOCIAL ACTION / SOCIAL 'MOVEMENT'; THE PERSON IS NOT THE PROBLEM, THE PROBLEM IS THE PROBLEM]

They (singular)

The American Dialect Society (2016) voted for 'they' used as a gender-neutral singular pronoun as their word of the year in 2015.

'Some have a fixed sense of their gender, for others it is more fluid.'

Meg-John Barker

Transfeminine transfemme

Terms used to describe transgender people who were assigned male at birth, but identify with femininity to a greater extent than with masculinity.

Transgender Trans

> Trans, or transgender, is a broad umbrella term for all those who do not remain in the gender that was assumed when they were born. Some may express their gender only at certain times or in certain contexts, others full time. Some may express their gender publicly, through names, pronouns, appearance, documents, etc. (known as social transition), others may not. Some may go through hormonal, surgical and/or other physical procedures to align their body with their gender (known as medical transition), others may not. Some have a fixed sense of their gender, for others it is more fluid. (Barker, 2018, p. 22)

[See MISGENDERING; PRONOUNS] .

Transmasculine transmasc

Terms used to describe transgender people who were assigned female at birth, but identify with masculinity to a greater extent than with femininity.

Transparency

A term originally suggested by David Epston as a counter point to the commonly accepted idea that for therapy to have its desired effects its workings need to be kept secret:

> The therapist can call into question the idea that s/he possesses an objective and unbiased account of reality, and undermine the possibility that persons will be subject to the imposition of ideas, by encouraging persons to interview her/him about the interview. In response to this, the therapist is able to deconstruct and thus embody her/his responses (including questions, comments, thoughts, and opinions) by situating these in the context of his/her personal experiences, imagination, and intentional states. This can be described as a condition of transparency in the therapeutic system, and it contributes to a context in which persons are more able to decide, for themselves, how they might take these therapist responses. (White, 1991, pp. 37–38)

[See OUTSIDER WITNESS; DISEMBODIED SPEECH]

Transphobia

Refers to negative beliefs, prejudices and stereotypes that exist about transgender and gender diverse people. Some, including Tiffany Sostar, appreciate the term transantagonism:

> I tend to use the term transantagonism more often than transphobia, because I appreciate how it highlights the ways in which many anti-trans actions (whether microaggressions or macro) are explicitly antagonistic, and result in so much harm. (Personal communication, 3rd February 2019)

Tree of Life narrative approach

The first metaphoric or folk cultural narrative practice, developed by Ncazelo Ncube-Mlilo (REPSSI – Regional Psychosocial Support Initiative) and David Denborough (Dulwich Centre Foundation). This approach seeks to use tree and natural metaphors to enable people to address the effects of 'trauma'/harm without having to speak directly, in the first person, about such harms. One of the reasons for its development was to contribute to democratising the field of narrative practice: to create a form of practice that could be put to use by concerned community members in Southern and Eastern Africa who may not have had access to professional education. (Ncube, 2006; Denborough 2008; 2018b)

Two Spirit

'Two Spirit identity is about circling back to where we belong, reclaiming, reinventing and redefining our beginnings, our roots, our communities, our support systems and our collective and individual selves.' Alex Wilson

In 1990, Myra Laramee coined the term Two Spirit, which was adopted at a gathering of native American and Canadian LGBTQ people in Manitoba. Some indigenous people choose to identify as Two Spirit rather than, or in addition to, identifying as lesbian, gay, bisexual, trans or queer. Prior to European arrival, Two Spirit people were respected members of their communities and were often accorded special status based on their unique abilities to understand both male and female perspectives. These identities were recognized and celebrated from a young age as gifts from the creator; Two Spirit people were often the visionaries, healers and medicine people. The term Two Spirit affirms the interrelatedness of all aspects of identity – including gender, sexuality, community, culture, and spirituality. It is an English term used to stand in for the many indigenous words for those with sexual and gender diverse identities. Many Two Spirit and their teachings were lost due to the impacts of colonization. An understanding of the complexities of Two Spirit people, builds wisdom in understanding their culture and intersectionality. (Egale Canada Human Rights Trust, 2018)

[See SISTERGIRL/BROTHERBOY]

Two-way account of therapy

Therapeutic interaction is a two-way phenomenon. We get together with people for a period of time over a range of issues, and all of our lives are changed for this. On some occasions these therapeutic interactions change our lives more significantly than on other occasions. When we are consulted by people who have survived abuse, and who are challenging the effects of this abuse in their lives, we are personally confronted to challenge much of what we have felt bound by in our own lives. Those people who are determined to break from the effects of various abuses that they have been subject to demonstrate a radical responsibility for the choices that they make about the discontinuities and the continuities of their lives. These choices about discontinuities are witnessed in their refusal to visit on others the abuses that have been visited on them, and in their determination to dispossess those who have perpetrated the abuse of the 'last say' in matters of personal identity. These choices about continuities are witnessed in their life-long determination to keep alive those precious sparks of hope – the hope that things might be different at some future time – despite the absolute discouragement of this, and in their maintenance of a fierce allegiance to whatever it is that has seen them through the dark hours of their lives.

In being privy to the performance of this radical responsibility for one's choices in life, we cannot be so resigned to the 'received' versions of our own lives. We are personally confronted with a whole range of choices about the continuities and the discontinuities of our own lives, and by the responsibility that we have to honour the invitation that these people are extending to us – to walk with them and to join them in making it our business to expose and to challenge the injustices of our world in whatever situations we find ourselves. (White, 1995e, pp. 7–8) u

U

Unexpected solidarities

Collective narrative practice, when involving exchanges of letters or documents between diverse groups, can at times lead to unanticipated moments of resonance across difference, or unexpected solidarities (see Denborough, 2018c).

Unique outcomes

Aspects of lived experience that fall outside the dominant story can be referred to as 'unique outcomes'. Unique outcomes contradict aspects of the problem-saturated description of individual/family/community life. Within narrative practice, they provide points of entry into alternative storylines of identity:

> I have borrowed this term from Goffman (1961). Steve de Shazer and his colleagues at the Brief Family Therapy Center in Milwaukee prefer 'exceptions' and the terms are interchangeable. The idea of exceptions produces 'exceptional persons' and that of unique outcomes produces 'unique persons'. Both are a joy to work with. (White, 1988b, p. 37)

Unrecognised networks

Michael White (1995e) emphasised the importance of acknowledging those mostly unrecognised networks that people go about building for themselves with others whom they strongly identify with. This acknowledgement of unrecognised or 'illegitimate' networks is especially significant for those who are considered marginal, those who, in Goffman's terms, have experienced 'spoiled identities':

> An example: I was recently consulted by a solemn young man who talked of his 'psychiatric history', and who, midway through the consultation, presented me with a rather grimy and slightly tattered letter. As I read this document aloud, the young man started to cry. I recognised the content of the letter. This was a 'document of identity' that I had assisted another young man, whom I will call James, also with a 'psychiatric history', to put together some eighteen months previously – only the name and the signature at the bottom had been changed. The young man and I talked about how he had come by the document, his identification with it, the circumstances under which James had encouraged him to substitute his own name, the generosity of this gesture, and about what this had meant to him. I then understood that this young man was crying for himself, and that these were tears of compassion, tears of a sort that, until this time, he had never been able to spill on his own behalf. And I learned from this young man that, in expressing this, he experienced James and many other young people crying with him, and that this provided a sense of community that was sustaining of him. Together, and with some joy, we began to plan some steps that we thought might bring acknowledgement to those people in this 'other' support network for the contributions that they were making to each other's lives. (White, 1995e, pp. 6–7)

Usable past

A term originally proposed by Wertsch (2002, p. 45) that is drawn upon by David Denborough to explain how narrative practices enable a re-engagement of history and the generation of a heritage of achievement that then makes future preferred action more possible:

> The process of collective documentation influences the collective memory of a group/community. Eliciting the principles, skills, and knowledge that are significant to community members, tracing the histories of these, and then re-telling, documenting, singing, and performing stories about this produces a particular form of 'social memory' (Popular Memory Group, 1998, p. 78). This social or shared memory links the actions of those in the present to the actions of those in the past. Significantly, this does not generate a nostalgic vision of the past, one that is separate from the actions or dilemmas of the present. Instead, these stories start in the present and then travel backwards. They historicise the skills, values, and knowledges that are being used to respond to current hardship. In doing so, this method of historicising can play a part in 'creating a usable past' (Wertsch, 2002, p. 45). The past becomes more available to draw upon in order to sustain present efforts. Remembering is a 'form of action' (Wertsch, 2002, p. 17). When what is collectively remembered are the ancestral contributions to current responses to social suffering, this form of remembrance can be 'like a medicine'. What's more, this 'usable past' then provides a foundation for further action in the present. A rich 'textual heritage' provides the basis for many more responses to current hardship, and the creation of many more stories. This process of creating a 'usable past' may be particularly significant in circumstances in which communities are being told by outsiders that their past is a burden, an obstacle to engaging with the 'real' mainstream world. (Denborough, Wingard, & White, 2009, p. 25)

[See POSITIVELY IMPLICATING PARENTS]

W

W

Welcome to country

There are long traditions of First Nations people of Australia seeking permission and granting permission to enter another Nation's traditional land. Aunty Joy Murphy Wandin describes this Welcome to Country process as it was practiced by the Wurundjeri:

> (Welcoming people to Country) is … paying respect, in a formal sense, and following traditional custom in a symbolic way.
>
> When there was a request to visit Country, the Werrigerri (a young man selected by the Elders of the community) would go on behalf of the community under the voice of the Elder, the Nurungeeta. There would be this negotiation and that could take a long time, it could take months. Everything could take a long time in traditional Aboriginal culture …
>
> When agreement was reached with the Wurundjeri, when you came to Country, first of all you must accept the law of the land, and that was about respect that contained all things.
>
> The other thing was that you could only stay for a short time. Why … ? Because our people were seasonal travellers … you knew what resources were available, you knew how to get them, you knew how long they would last. So that staying here with us was about sharing … but sharing it with your neighbouring community that could be twice your size was a big effort.
>
> The traditional ceremonies were quite big. The Yarnabool (visiting communities) would come with bark torches in their hand … to cleanse that journey, 'swept away' as my mother would say. And so when they came onto Country there (was) a set up of two fires, and the eucalyptus around were used as gifts … Then the two Nurungeetas would come together at the fires, they would exchange whatever was necessary … and then there would be a big celebration … It was a very long process and a very beautiful process.

‘Welcome to country … is paying respect, especially to our ancestors.’

Aunty Joy Murphy

Welcome to country *(continued)*

So that is the background of Welcome to Country. It is not a new thing. It is not … because our land was dispossessed; it has nothing to do with that. It is all about respect for our culture and who we are. It is paying respect, especially to our ancestors. (Australians Together, 2019)

A Welcome to Country is delivered at the beginning of a formal event by Traditional Owners, or Aboriginal and Torres Strait Islander people who have been given permission from Traditional Owners, to welcome visitors to their Country. For more information, and to consider the difference between a ‘Welcome to Country’ and an ‘Acknowledgement of Country’, see: Reconciliation Australia (n.d.).

Woman

Whether trans or cisgender, intersex or not, many people identify as women. However, what this means varies a great deal depending on their other intersecting attributes. It is important not to assume, for example, that being a woman necessarily involves being able to bear children, or having XX sex chromosomes, or breasts. (Barker, 2018, p. 25)

Womanism

[See BLACK FEMINISM]

y

Yarning as spiritual practice

Tileah Drahm-Butler (2015):

> If narrative practice is to be part of a decolonising process then the recognition of spirituality within yarning about identity will be significant. Connection to cultural stories is a spiritual practice. Understanding the interconnectedness of people within kinship systems and of people with Land and the cosmos is therefore a key part of this work (Laycock et al. 2011).

'If narrative practice is to be part of a decolonising process then the recognition of spirituality within yarning about identity will be significant.'

Tileah Drahm-Butler

References

Aboriginal Health Council of South Australia. (1995). Reclaiming our stories, reclaiming our lives. *Dulwich Centre Newsletter*, 1, 1–40.

Abu-Rayyan, N. M. (2009). Seasons of Life: Ex-detainees reclaiming their lives. *International Journal of Narrative Practice and Community Work*, 2, 24–40.

Adams, F. & Horton, M. (1975). *Unearthing seeds of fire: The idea of Highlander*. North Carolina: John F. Blair Publisher.

Adichie, C. (2009). The danger of a single story. TED. London. *You Tube*. Retrieved from http://www.youtube.com/watch?v=D9Ihs241zeg.

Akinyela, M. (2002). De-colonizing our lives. Divining a post-colonial therapy. *International Journal of Narrative Therapy and Community Work*, 2, 32–43.

Allen, A. (1996). Foucault on power: a theory for feminists. In Hekman, S. J. (Ed.). *Feminist interpretations of Michel Foucault* (pp. 265–282). University Park, PA: Penn State University Press.

American Dialect Society (2016). 2015 Word of the Year is singular 'they'. Retrieved from https://www.americandialect.org/2015-word-of-the-year-is-singular-they

Ansara, Y. G. (2013). Misgendering is a mental health issue. In National LGBTI Health Alliance (March 2013) *LGBTI Health Update* Volume 3, Issue 2. Sydney, Australia. Retrieved from https://www.lgbtihealth.org.au/sites/default/files/LGBTIHealthUpdate-March2013_0.pdf.

Arab American National Museum, (2011). *Reclaiming Identity: Dismantling Arab Stereotypes*. Retrieved from http://www.arabstereotypes.org/why-stereotypes/what-orientalism Downloaded 8 January 2019.

Australians Together, (2019). Understanding Welcome to Country. Retrieved from https://australianstogether.org.au/discover/indigenous-culture/understanding-welcome-to-country/

Avery, S. (2018). *Culture is inclusion: A narrative of Aboriginal and Torres Strait Islander people with disability*. Sydney, Australia: First Peoples Disability Network

Barenboim, D. & Said, E. (2004). *Parallels and paradoxes: Explorations in music and society*. London, UK: Bloomsbury Publishing.

Barker, M-J, (2018). *Good Practice across the Counselling Professions 001 Gender, Sexual, and Relationship Diversity* (GSRD). Leicestershire, UK: British Association for Counselling and Psychotherapy.

Barker, M-J. & Scheele, J. (2016). *Queer: A graphic history*. London, UK: Icon Books.

Bateson, G. (1980). *Mind and nature: A necessary unity*. New York, NY: Bantam Books.

References
(continued)

Benestad, E. E. P. (2016). Gender belonging: Children, adolescents, adults and the role of the therapist – Revised. *International Journal of Narrative Therapy and Community Work*, 4, 91–106.

Berghs, M., Atkin, K., Graham, H., Hatton, C., & Thomas, C. (2016). Implications for public health research of models and theories of disability: a scoping study and evidence synthesis. *Public Health Research*, (4) 8.

Berne, P., Milbern, S. & Weiner-Mahfuz, L. (n.d.). Disability justice: New intersections between race, justice & disability. Retrieved from https://www.sinsinvalid.org/PDFs/DJBriefing_Powerpoint.pdf.

Bourdieu, P. (1988). *Homo Academicus*. Redwood City, California: Stanford University Press.

Brigitte, Sue, Mem & Veronika, (1997). Power to our journeys. *Dulwich Centre Newsletter*, No.1. First published in the 1996 Summer edition of the AFTA Newsletter. Republished 1998 in C. White & D. Denborough (eds): *Introducing Narrative Therapy: A collection of practice-based writings* (chapter 13), pp. 203–215. Adelaide, Australia: Dulwich Centre Publications.

Bruner, E. (2005). *Culture on tour: Ethnographies of travel*. Chicago, IL: University of Chicago Press.

Bruner, J. (1986). *Actual Minds, Possible Worlds*. Cambridge, Mass: Harvard University Press.

Bullimore, P. (2003). Altering the balance of power: working with voices. *International Journal of Narrative Therapy and Community Work*, 3, 22–28.

Chandler, D. & Munday, R. (Eds.). (2016). A Dictionary of Media and Communication (online version) Oxford, UK: Oxford University Press. Retrieved from http://www.oxfordreference.com/view/10.1093/oi/authority.20110803095507973 on 8 Jan 2019.

Child Family Community Australia, (2017). LGBTIQ+ communities: Glossary of common terms. Retrieved from https://aifs.gov.au/cfca/publications/lgbtiq-communities

Chomsky. N. & Foucault, M. (2011) [1974]. Human Nature: Justice versus Power. The Chomsky-Foucault debate (Edited by Fons Elders). London, UK: Souvenir Press.

Chrystos, (2003). An interview with Chrystos by Joanne Bealy. *Off Our Backs*, September-October.

Clemens, C. (2017). Ally or accomplice? The language of activism. Retrieved from https://www.tolerance.org/magazine/ally-or-accomplice-the-language-of-activism

Code, L. (Ed.) (2000). *Encyclopedia of Feminist Theories*. New York, NY: Routledge.

Cole, N. L. (2018, January 16). What Is Discourse? Retrieved from https://thoughtco.com/discourse-definition-3026070.

Connell, R. W. (1995). *Masculinities*. Sydney, Australia: Allen & Unwin

Costas, J., & Flemming, P. (2009). Beyond dis-identification: A discursive approach to self-alienation in contemporary organizations. *Human Relations*, 62(3), 353–378.

Crenshaw, K. W. (1989). Demarginalizing the intersection of race and sex: A Black Feminist critique of antidiscrimination doctrine, feminist theory and antiracist politics. *University of Chicago Legal Forum, special issue: Feminism in the Law: Theory, Practice and Criticism*, (pp. 139–168). Chicago, IL: University of Chicago Law School.

Davis, A. Y. (2005). *Abolition democracy: Beyond empire, prisons, and torture*. New York, NY: Seven Stories Press.

References
(continued)

Denborough, D. (1995a). Becoming squarehead, becoming gubba. In D. Denborough (Ed.) *Beyond the prison: Gathering dreams of freedom*, (pp. 111–125). Adelaide, Australia: Dulwich Centre Publications.

Denborough, D. (Ed.) (1995b). *Beyond the prison: Gathering dreams of freedom*. Adelaide, Australia: Dulwich Centre Publications.

Denborough, D. (2002a). *The Narrandera Koori Community Gathering*. Retrieved from https://dulwichcentre.com.au/articles-about-narrative-therapy/narrandera/

Denborough, D. (2002b). Community song writing and narrative practice. *Clinical Psychology*, 17, 17–24.

Denborough, D. (2006). A framework for receiving and documenting testimonies of trauma. In D. Denborough (Ed.), *Trauma: Narrative responses to traumatic experience* (pp. 115–131). Adelaide, Australia: Dulwich Centre Publications. (Reprinted from *International Journal of Narrative Therapy and Community Work*, 2005, 3&4, 34–42.)

Denborough, D. (2008). *Collective narrative practice: Responding to individuals, groups and communities who have experienced trauma*. Adelaide, Australia: Dulwich Centre Publications.

Denborough, D. (2010a). *Kite of Life: From intergenerational conflict to intergenerational alliance.* Adelaide, Australia: Dulwich Centre Foundation. Denborough, D. (2010b). *Working with memory in the shadow of genocide: The narrative practices of Ibuka trauma counsellors.* Adelaide, Australia: Dulwich Centre Foundation International.

Denborough, D. (2010b). *Working with memory in the shadow of genocide: The narrative practices of Ibuka trauma counsellors*. Adelaide, Australia: Dulwich Centre Foundation International.

Denborough, D. (2014). *Retelling the stories of our lives: Everyday narrative therapy to draw inspiration and transform experience.* New York, NY: W. W. Norton.

Denborough, D. (2018). *Do you want to hear a story? Adventures in collective narrative practice.* Adelaide, Australia: Dulwich Centre Publications.

Denborough, D. (2018a). 'Gathering up courage': Can narrative practice play a part in sustaining activism and human rights work? In D. Denborough, *Do you want to hear a story? Adventures in collective narrative practice* (pp. 119–137). Adelaide, Australia: Dulwich Centre Publications.

Denborough, D. (2018b). Tracing the roots of the Tree of Life narrative approach. In D. Denborough, *Do you want to hear a story? Adventures in collective narrative practice* (pp. 57–75). Adelaide, Australia: Dulwich Centre Publications.

Denborough, D. (2018c). Unexpected solidarities: 'We've got to work together'. In D. Denborough, *Do you want to hear a story? Adventures in collective narrative practice* (pp. 5–21). Adelaide, Australia: Dulwich Centre Publications.

Denborough, D. (in press). Travelling down the neuro-pathway: Narrative practice, neuroscience, bodies, emotions and the affective turn. *International Journal of Narrative Therapy and Community Work.*

Denborough, D., Freedman, J., & White, C. (2008). *Strengthening resistance: The use of narrative practices in working with genocide survivors.* Adelaide, Australia: Dulwich Centre Foundation.

Denborough, D., Koolmatrie, C., Mununggirritj, D., Marika, D., Dhurrkay, W. & Yunupingu, M. (2006). Linking stories and initiatives: A narrative approach to working with the skills and knowledge of communities. *International Journal of Narrative Therapy and Community Work*, 2, 19–51.

References *(continued)*

Denborough, D., Wingard, B., & White, C. (2009). *Yia Marra: Good stories that make spirits strong – from the people of Ntaria/Hermannsburg.* Adelaide and Alice Springs, Australia: Dulwich Centre Publications and General Practice Network NT.

Derrida, J. (1978). *Writing and difference.* Chicago, IL: University of Chicago Press.

Derrida, J. (2016). *Of grammatology* (G. T. Spivak, Trans.). Baltimore, MA: Johns Hopkins University Press. (Original work published 1967)

de Valda, M. (2003). From paranoid schizophrenia to hearing voices – and other class distinctions. *International Journal of Narrative Therapy and Community Work*, 3, 13–17.

Dowse, K. (2017). Thwarting Shame: Feminist engagement in group work with men recruited to patriarchal dominance in relationship. *International Journal of Narrative Therapy and Community Work*, 1, 1–9.

Drahm-Butler, T. (2015). Decolonising identity stories: Narrative practice through Aboriginal eyes. In B. Wingard, C. Johnson, & T. Drahm-Butler, *Aboriginal narrative practice: Honouring storylines of pride, strength and creativity* (pp. 25–46). Adelaide, Australia: Dulwich Centre Publications.

DuBois, W.E.B. (1903/1989). *The Souls of Black Folk.* New York, NY: Bantam Books.

Egale Canada Human Rights Trust (2018). Two spirits one voice. Retrieved from https://egale.ca/portfolio/two-spirits-one-voice/

Eisner, S. (2013). The difference between monosexism and biphobia. Retrieved from https://radicalbi.wordpress.com/2013/02/08/the-difference-between-monosexism-and-biphobia

Epston, D. (1999). Co-research: The making of an alternative knowledge. In Dulwich Centre (Ed.), *Narrative therapy and community work: A conference collection* (pp. 137–157). Adelaide, Australia: Dulwich Centre Publications.

Epston, D. (2001). Anthropology, archives, co-research and narrative therapy. In D. Denborough (Ed.), *Family therapy: Exploring the field's past, present and possible futures* (pp. 177–182). Adelaide, Australia: Dulwich Centre Publications.

Epston, D. (2014). Ethnography, co-research and insider knowledges. *Australian and New Zealand Journal of Family Therapy, 35*(1), 105–109.

Epston, D. & Maisel, R. (2009). Anti-anorexia/bulimia: A polemics of life and death. In H. Malson & M. Burns (Eds.), *Critical feminist approaches to eating dis/orders*, London, UK: Routledge.

Epston, D., Morris, F. & Maisel, R. (1995). A narrative approach to so-called anorexia/bulimia. In K. Weingarten (Ed.), *Cultural resistance: Challenging beliefs about men, women and therapy* (pp. 69–96). New York, NY: Harrington Park Press.

Fanon, F. (1961). *The wretched of the Earth.* New York, NY: Grove Press.

Fileborn, B. (2012). Sexual violence and gay, lesbian, bisexual, trans, intersex, and queer communities. *Australian Centre for the Study of Sexual Assault (ACSSA) Resource Sheet.* Melbourne, Australia: Australian Institute of Family Studies. Retrieved from www3.aifs.gov.au/acssa/pubs/sheets/rs3/.

Findlay, R. (2016). Five radical ideas, splits and things not to leave behind (Interviewer Cheryl White). In C. White (Ed.), *A memory book for the field of narrative practice* (pp. 19–25). Adelaide, Australia: Dulwich Centre.

References

(continued)

Foucault, M. (1975). *Discipline and punish: The birth of the prison*. New York, NY: Random House.

Foucault, M. (1980). 'Two Lectures' in C. Gordon (Ed.), Power/knowledge: Selected interviews and other writings 1972-1977, (pp. 78–108). New York, NY: Pantheon.

Foucault, M. (1983). Afterword. In H. L. Dreyfus, & P. Rabinow (Eds.), *Michael Foucault: Beyond structuralism and hermeneutics* (pp. 208–252). Chicago, IL: University of Chicago Press.

Foucault, M. (1984). What is Enlightenment. In P. Rabinow (Ed.), *The foucault reader* (pp. 32–50). New York, NY: Pantheon Books.

Foucault, M. (1988a). The ethic of care for the self as a practice of freedom. In J. Bernauer & D. Rasmussen (Eds.), *The Final Foucault*. Cambridge, MA: The MIT Press.

Foucault, M. (1988b). Technologies of the self. In L. Martin, H. Gutman & P. Hutton (Eds.), *Technologies of the Self.* Amherst: University of Massachusetts Press.

Foucault, M. (1988c). Power, Moral Values, and the Intellectual (Interviewer Michael Bess). *History of the Present* 4 (1) 11–13. Retrieved from https://www.michaelbess.org/foucault-interview/

Foucault, M. (2012). *The archaeology of knowledge*. New York, NY: Vintage.

Freer, M. (1997). Taking a defiant stand against sexual abuse and the mother-blaming discourse. *Gecko: A journal of deconstruction and narrative ideas in therapeutic practice*, 1, 5–28.

Freire, P. (1970). *Pedagogy of the Oppressed*. New York, NY: Herder and Herder.

Freire, P. (1994). *Pedagogy of hope: Reliving Pedagogy of the oppressed*. New York, NY: Continuum.

Garland-Thomson, R. (2006). Integrating disability, transforming feminist theory, in L. J. Davis (Ed.), *The disability studies reader*, (pp. 257–274). New York, NY: Taylor & Francis.

Geia L. K., Hayes, B. & Usher, K. (2013). Yarning/Aboriginal storytelling: towards an understanding of an Indigenous perspective and its implications for research practice. *Contemporary Nurse*. Dec; 46(1):13–7. doi: 10.5172/conu.2013.46.1.13.

Goffman, E. (1961). *Asylums: Essays on the Condition of the Social Situation of Mental Patients and Other Inmates*. Harmondsworth, UK: Penguin Books.

Golder, B. (2015). *Foucault and the politics of rights*. Stanford, California: Stanford University Press.

Gorrie, N. & Church, W. (2018). We need to abolish prisons to disrupt a society built on inequality. Retrieved from https://www.theguardian.com/commentisfree/2018/nov/26/we-need-to-abolish-prisons-to-disrupt-a-society-built-on-inequality

Grieves, L. (1997). From beginning to start: The Vancouver Anti-Anorexia Anti-Bulimia League. *Gecko: A Journal of Deconstruction and Narrative Ideas in Therapeutic Practice*, 2, 78–88.

Hall, R. (1994). Partnership accountability. *Dulwich Centre Newsletter*, 2&3, 6–29.

Hammoud-Beckett, S. (2007). Azima ila Hayati – An invitation in to my life: Narrative conversations about sexual identity. *International Journal of Narrative Therapy and Community Work*, 1, 29–39.

Hanisch, C. (1970). The personal is political. In S. Firestone & A. Koedt (Eds.), *Notes from the second year: Women's Liberation, major writings of the radical feminists* (pp. 76–78). New York, NY: Radical Feminism.

References *(continued)*

Haraway, D. (1988). Situated knowledges: The science question in feminism and the privilege of partial perspective. *Feminist Studies 14*(3), 575–599.

Hare-Mustin, R. T. (1978). A feminist approach to family therapy. *Family Process*, 17, 181–194.

Hare-Mustin, R. T. (1987). The problem of gender in family therapy theory. *Family Process*, 26, 15–27.

Hare-Mustin, R. T. & Marecek, J. (1990). *Making a Difference: Psychology and the construct of gender.* New Haven, CT: Yale University Press.

Hare-Mustin, R. (2001). Thinking differently about gender. In Dulwich Centre (Ed.), *Working with the Stories of Women's Lives.* Adelaide, Australia: Dulwich Centre Publications.

Hekman, S. (Ed.) (1996). *Feminist Interpretations of Michel Foucault.* Pennsylvania, USA: Pennsylvania State University Press.

Heath, M. (2012). On critical thinking. *International Journal of Narrative Therapy and Community Work*, 4, 11–18.

Heron, B. (2005). Self-reflection in critical social work practice: subjectivity and the possibilities of resistance, *Reflective Practice*, (6)3, 341-351.

Hewson, D. (2002). Heterosexual dominance in the world of therapy? In D. Denborough (Ed.), *Queer Counselling and Narrative Practice* (pp. 52–62). Adelaide, Australia: Dulwich Centre Publications. (Reprinted from *Dulwich Centre Newsletter*, 1993, 2, 14–20).

hooks, b. (2000). Consciousness-raising: A constant change of heart. In b. hooks (Ed.), *Feminism is for everybody: Passionate politics* (pp. 7–12). Cambridge, MA: South End.

Hoosain, S. (2013). The transmission of intergenerational trauma in displaced families. PhD thesis, Department of Social Work, University of the Western Cape, South Africa.

Horton, M. & Freire, P. (1990). *We make the road by walking: Conversations on education and social change* (Eds. B. Bell, J. Gaventa & J. Peters). Philadelphia, PA: Temple University Press.

Hutton, J. (2008). Turning the spotlight back on the normalising gaze. *International Journal of Narrative Therapy and Community Work*, 1, 3–16.

James, K. (2001). Feminist reflections on family therapy and working on the issue of men's violence. An interview in D. Denborough (Ed.), *Family Therapy: Exploring the field's past, present & possible futures.* Adelaide, Australia: Dulwich Centre Publications.

James, K. & McIntyre, D. (1983). The reproduction of families: The social role of family therapy? *Journal of Marital Family Therapy*, 9, 119–129.

James, W. (1892). *Psychology: Brief course.* London, UK: Macmillan.

Jenkins, A. (1990). *Invitations to responsibility: The therapeutic engagement of men who are violent and abusive.* Adelaide, Australia: Dulwich Centre Publications.

Jones, S. R. (2013). *No you don't: Essays from an unstrange mind.* Florida, USA: Unstrange Publications.

Kafer, A. (2013). *Feminist, Queer, Crip*, Bloomington, IN: Indiana University Press.

Kaminsky, M. (1992). Introduction. In B. Myerhoff & M. Kaminsky (Ed.), *Remembered lives: the work of ritual, storytelling, and growing older.* University of Michigan Press: Ann Arbor.

References *(continued)*

Kamsler, A. (1990). Her-story in the making: Therapy with women who were sexually abused in childhood. In M. Durrant & C. White (Eds.), *Ideas for therapy with sexual abuse* (pp. 9-36). Adelaide, Australia: Dulwich Centre Publications.

Kapitan, A. (2017). The radical copyeditor's style guide for writing about transgender people. Retrieved from https://radicalcopyeditor.com/2017/08/31/transgender-style-guide/

Kaplan, M (1983). A woman's view of DSM-III. *American Psychologist*, July, 786–92.

Kidner, D. W. (1996). Why psychology is mute about the environmental crisis. *Environmental Ethics*, 16(4): 359–376.

King, J. (2015, June 25). Meet the trans women of color who helped put Stonewall Inn on the map. Retrieved from https://mic.com/articles/121256/meet-marsha-p-johnson-and-sylvia-rivera-transgender-stonewall-veterans#.vJ5maNTtW

Kitzinger, C. & Perkins, R. (1993). *Changing our minds: Lesbian feminism and psychology.* New York, NY: New York University Press.

Kramarae, C. & Treichler, P. A. (1985). *A feminist dictionary*. London, UK: Pandora Press.

Kunc, N., Van der Klift, E., Reynolds, V. & Munro, A. (2015). Relocating the problem of disability. Retrieved from https://dulwichcentre.com.au/relocating-the-problem-of-disability-norm-kunc-emma-van-der-klift-vikki-reynolds-and-aaron-munro/

Lainson, K. (2016). From 'disorder' to political action: Conversations that invite collective considerations to individual experiences of women who express concerns about eating and their bodies. *International Journal of Narrative Therapy and Community Work*, 2, 1–15.

Laycock, A., Walker, D., Harrison, N. & Brands, J. (2011). *Researching Indigenous health: A practical guide for researchers.* Melbourne, Australia: The Lowitja Institute.

Leonard, W., Mitchell, A., Patel, S., & Fox, C. (2008). *Coming forward: The underreporting of heterosexist violence and same sex partner abuse in Victoria.* Bundoora, Australia: Australian Research Centre in Sex, Health and Society.

Living positive lives: A gathering for people with an HIV positive diagnosis and workers within the HIV sector. (2000). *Dulwich Centre Journal*, 4.

Lock, A., Epston, D. & Maisel, R. (2004). Countering that which is called anorexia. *Narrative Inquiry, 14*(2), 275–301.

Lock, A., Epston, D., Maisel, R. & de Faria, N. (2005). Resisting anorexia/bulimia: Foucauldian perspectives in narrative therapy, *British Journal of Guidance and Counselling, 33*(3), 315–332.

Madigan, S. (2010). New forms of writing and naming – Therapeutic letter writing campaigns. Retrieved from http://therapeuticconversations.com/wp-content/uploads/2010/01/Handout_Madigan_TC9_letters.pdf.

Madigan, S. (2019). *Narrative therapy.* Washington, DC, US: American Psychological Association.

Madigan, S. & Epston, D. (1995). From 'spy-chiatric' gaze to communities of concern: From professional monologue to dialogue. In S. Friedman (Ed.), *The reflecting team in action: Collaborative practice in family therapy* (pp. 257–276). New York, NY: Guilford Publications.

References
(continued)

Maeder, R. & Dulwich Centre, (2018). She/he/they/ze: Talking about *pronouns* and *gendered language*. Adelaide, Australia, Dulwich Centre. Retrieved from *www.dulwichcentre.com.au/misgendering*

Maisel, R., Epston, D. & Borden, A. (2004). *Biting the hand that starves you: Inspiring resistance to anorexia/bulimia*. New York, NY: W. W. Norton.

Malson, H. & Burns, M. (Eds.) (2009). *Critical and feminist approaches to disordered eating*, London, UK: Routledge.

McGoldrick, M., Anderson, C.M. & Walsh, F. (eds) 1989: Women in Families: *A framework for family therapy*. New York, NY: W. W. Norton.

McLaren, M. (2002). *Feminism, Foucault, and embodied subjectivity*. Albany, NY: State University of New York Press.

McMenamin, D. (1999). Interviewing racism. In Dulwich Centre Publications (Eds.), *Extending narrative therapy: A collection of practice-based papers* (pp. 13–19). Adelaide, Australia: Dulwich Centre Publications. (Reprinted from *Dulwich Centre Journal*, 1998, 1&2, 42–44)

McNay, L. (1992). Foucault and feminism: Power, gender, and the self. Cambridge, UK: Polity Press.

Morgan (2000). *When chickenheads come home to roost: My life as a hip-hop feminist*. New York, NY: Simon & Shuster

Myerhoff, B. (1982). Life history among the elderly: Performance, visibility, and re-membering. In J. Ruby (Ed.), *A crack in the mirror: Reflective perspectives in anthropology* (pp. 99–117). Philadelphia, PA: University of Pennsylvania Press.

Myerhoff, B. (1986). 'Life not death in Venice': Its second life. In V. Turner & E. Bruner (Eds.), *The anthropology of experience* (pp. 261–286). Chicago, IL: University of Illinois Press.

Ncube, N. (2006). The Tree of Life Project: Using narrative ideas in work with vulnerable children in Southern Africa. *International Journal of Narrative Therapy and Community Work*, 1, 3–16.

Neighbouring Communities Project (2007). Retrieved from http://www.briefnarrative.com/projects/neighbouring-communities.html

Nelson, H. L. (2001). *Damaged identities, narrative repair*. Ithaca, NY; Cornell University Press.

Nicholls, C. & North, I. (2001). *Kathleen Petyarre: Genius of place*. Adelaide, Australia: Wakefield Press.

Piepzna-Samarasinha, L. L (2018). *Care work: Dreaming disability justice*. Vancouver, Canada: Arsenal Pulp Press.

Prilleltensky, I. (1994). *The morals and politics of psychology: Psychological discourse and the status quo*. New York: State University of New York.

Raheim, S., White, C., Denborough, D., Waldegrave, C., Tamasese, K., Tuhaka, F., Franklin, A., Fox, H. & Carey, M. (2004). An invitation to narrative practitioners to address privilege and dominance. Retrieved from www.dulwichcentre.com.au/a-continuing-invitation-to-narrative-practitioners-to-address-privilege-and-dominance/

Reconciliation Australia (n.d.) Welcome to and Acknowledgement of Country. Retrieved from https://www.reconciliation.org.au/wp-content/uploads/2017/11/Welcome-to-and-Acknowledgement-of-Country.pdf

Redstockings Manifesto (1970). In R, Morgan (Ed.), *Sisterhood is Powerful* (pp. 533–5), New York, NY: Vintage.

References
(continued)

Reynolds, V. (2011). Resisting burnout with justice-doing. *International Journal of Narrative Therapy and Community Work*, 4, 27–45.

Reynolds, V. (2013). Centering ethics in group supervision: Fostering cultures of critique and structuring safety. *International Journal of Narrative Therapy and Community Work*, 4, 1–13.

Rigney, L. I. (1999). Internationalization of an Indigenous anticolonial cultural critique of research methodologies: A guide to Indigenist research methodology and its principles. *Wicazo Sa Review: A Journal of Native American Studies*, 14:2:109–121.

Roper, C., Grey, F. & Cadogan, E. (2018). Co-production: Putting principles into practice in mental health contexts. Retrieved from https://recoverylibrary.unimelb.edu.au/__data/assets/pdf_file/0010/2659969/Coproduction_putting-principles-into-practice.pdf

Roth, S., & Epston, D. (1996). Consulting the problem about the problematic relationship: An exercise for experiencing a relationship with an externalised problem. In M. Hoyt (Ed.), *Constructive therapies 2* (pp. 148–162). New York, NY: Guilford Press. Reprinted in D. Epston (1998), *'Catching up' with David Epston: A collection of narrative practice-based papers published between 1991 & 1996* (pp. 209–226). Adelaide, Australia: Dulwich Centre Publications.

Russell, S. & Carey, M. (2003). Feminism, therapy and narrative ideas: Exploring some not so commonly asked questions, *International Journal of Narrative Therapy and Community Work*, 2, 67–91.

Said, E. (1978). *Orientalism*. New York, NY: Pantheon Books

Salamone, F. A. (Ed.). (2004). *Encyclopedia of religious rites, rituals and festivals*. New York, NY: Routledge.

Sawicki, J. (1991). *Disciplining Foucault: Feminism, power, and the body*. New York, NY: Routledge.

Shenk, T (2015). Booked #3: What Exactly Is Neoliberalism? An interview with Wendy Brown. Retrieved from https://www.dissentmagazine.org/blog/booked-3-what-exactly-is-neoliberalism-wendy-brown-undoing-the-demos

Sliep, Y. (2005). A narrative theatre approach to working with communities affected by trauma, conflict and war, *International Journal of Narrative Therapy and Community Work*, 2, 47–52.

Sliep, Y. & CARE Counsellors. (1996). *Pang' ono pang' ono ndi mtolo* – little by little we make a bundle. *Dulwich Centre Newsletter*, (3), 3–11. Reprinted in C. White & D. Denborough (Eds.) (1998), *Introducing narrative therapy: A collection of practice-based writings* (pp. 141–156). Adelaide, Australia: Dulwich Centre Publications.

Sostar, T. (2018). Turning hopelessness into action: Narrative responses to the late-2018 political context (video). Retrieved from https://dulwichcentre.com.au/turning-hopelessness-into-action-narrative-responses-to-the-late-2018-political-context-by-tiffany-sostar/

Speaking out … and being heard. (1995). *Dulwich Centre Newsletter*, 4, 1–56.

Spencer, M., Dineen, R., & Phillips, A. (2013). Co-producing services – Co-creating health. Retrieved from http://www.1000livesplus.wales.nhs.uk/sitesplus/documents/1011/T4I%20%288%29%20Co%2Dproduction.pdf

Spivak, G. C. (1993). Can the subaltern speak? In L. Chrisman & P. Williams (Ed.). *Colonial discourse and post-colonial theory: a reader* (pp. 66–111). New York, NY: Harvester Wheatsheaf.

Stanley, J. P. (1974). The stylistics of belief. College Composition and Communication Conference, Anaheim, California.

References

(continued)

Stanley, J. P. (1975). Prescribed passivity: the language of sexism. In R. Ordoubadian & W. Von-Raffler Engel (Eds.), *Views on Language.* Murfreesboro, TN: Inter-University Publishing.

Sue, Mem & Veronika, (1999). Documents and treasures. Power To Our Journeys. In Dulwich Centre Publications (Eds.), *Narrative Therapy & Community Work: A conference collection* (pp. 115–124). Adelaide, Australia: Dulwich Centre Publications.

Tamasese, T. K. (2000). Talking about culture and gender: An interview with Kiwi Tamasese. In Dulwich Centre (Eds), *Working with the stories of women's lives* (pp. 15–21). Adelaide, Australia: Dulwich Centre Publications.

Tamasese, T. K. (2007). Working for gender justice across cultures: An interview with Taimalieutu Kiwi Tamasese (Interviewer C. White). In Yuen, A. & White, C. (Eds.), *Conversations about gender, culture, violence & narrative practice* (pp. 99–106). Adelaide, Australia: Dulwich Centre Publications.

Tamasese T. K., & Waldegrave, C. (1996). 'Cultural and Gender Accountability in the 'Just Therapy' Approach.' In Mclean, C. Carey, M., & White, C. (Eds.), *Men's Ways of Being.* Boulder, CO: Westview Press.

Tamasese, Waldegrave, Tuhaka & Campbell (1998). 'Furthering conversation about partnerships of accountability', *Dulwich Centre Journal*, 4, 50–64.

Thomas, L. (2002). Poststructuralism and therapy – what's it all about? *International Journal of Narrative Therapy and Community Work*, 2, 85–89.

Tilsen, J. & Nylund, D. (2010). Resisting normativity: Queer musings on politics, identity, and the performance of therapy. *International Journal of Narrative Therapy and Community Work*, 3, 64–70.

Trudinger, M. (2006). Maps of violence, maps of hope: Using place and maps to explore identity, gender, and violence. *International Journal of Narrative Therapy and Community Work*, 3: 11–42.

Tuck, E. (2009). Suspending Damage: A Letter to Communities. *Harvard Educational Review*, 79 (3), 409–427.

Tuck, E. & Yang, K. W. (2012). Decolonization is not a metaphor. *Decolonization: Indigeneity, Education & Society*, 1 (1), 1–40.

Turner, V. (1969). *The ritual process: Structure and anti-structure.* New York, NY: Aldine de Gruyter.

Turner, V. (1979). *Process, performance and pilgrimage: A study in comparative symbology.* New Delhi, India: Concept Publishing Company.

Turner, V. (1986). Dewey, Dilthey, and Drama: An essay in the anthropology of experience. In Turner, V. W. & Bruner, E. M. (Eds.), *The Anthropology of Experience.* Chicago, IL: University of Illinois Press.

Vizenor, G. (1991). *Manifest manners: Narratives on PostIndian Survivance.* Nebraska, USA: University of Nebraska Press.

Walia, H. (2013). *Undoing border imperialism.* Oakland, CA: AK Press.

Waldegrave, C. (2000). Grappling with a contemporary and inclusive spirituality, *Dulwich Centre Journal*, 1&2; 34–16. Reprinted in Waldegrave, C., Tamasese, K., Tuhaka, F., & Campbell, W. (Eds.) (2003), *Just Therapy – a journey: A collection of papers from the Just Therapy Team, New Zealand* (pp. 161–166). Adelaide, Australia: Dulwich Centre Publications.

References
(continued)

Waldegrave, C., Tamasese, K., Tuhaka, F., & Campbell, W. (Eds.) (2003), *Just Therapy – a journey: A collection of papers from the Just Therapy Team, New Zealand.* Adelaide, Australia: Dulwich Centre Publications.

Walters, M., Carter, B., Papp, P. & Silverstein, O. (1988). *The Invisible Web: Gender patterns in family relationships.* New York, NY: Guilford Press.

Warner, M. (1991). Fear of a queer planet. *Social Text, 29*, 3–17.

Watson, I. (2014). Re-centring First Nations knowledge and places in a Terra Nullius space. *Alternative* Vol., 10, Issue 5, 508–520.

Weedon, C. (1987). *Feminist practice and post-structuralist theory.* Oxford: Basil Blackwell.

Welch, S. (1990). *A feminist ethic of risk.* Minneapolis, MN: Fortress Press.

Wertsch, J. V. (2002). *Voices of collective remembering.* Cambridge, MA: Cambridge University Press.

Westoby, P. (2009). *The sociality of refugee healing: In dialogue with Southern Sudanese refugees resettling in Australia.* Champaign, IL: Common Ground.

White, C. (2016). *A memory book for the field of narrative practice.* Adelaide, Australia: Dulwich Centre Publications.

White, C., & Denborough, D. (2005). *A community of ideas: Behind the scenes: The work of Dulwich Centre Publications.* Adelaide, Australia: Dulwich Centre Publications.

White, M. (1988a). Saying hullo again: The incorporation of the lost relationship in the resolution of grief. *Dulwich Centre Newsletter*, Spring, 7–11. In C. White & D. Denborough (Eds.), *Introducing narrative therapy: A collection of practice-based writings* (pp. 17–29). Adelaide, Australia: Dulwich Centre Publications.

White, M. (1988b). The process of questioning: A therapy of literary merit? *Dulwich Centre Newsletter*, Winter, 8–14. Reprinted in M. White (1989), *Selected papers* (pp. 37–46). Adelaide, Australia: Dulwich Centre Publications.

White, M. (1989, November 5) *On Power and Foucault* [Video recording]. Michael White Video Archive (Tape 225). Adelaide, Australia: Dulwich Centre.

White, M. (1991). Deconstruction and therapy. *Dulwich Centre Newsletter*, 3:21–40. Reprinted in D. Epston, & M. White (1992), *Experience, Contradiction, Narrative & Imagination: Selected papers of David Epston & Michael White, 1989-1991* (pp. 109–151). Adelaide, Australia: Dulwich Centre Publications.

White, M. (1992). Men's culture, the men's movement, and the constitution of men's lives. *Dulwich Centre Newsletter,* 3&4, 33–53.

White, M. (1993). Histories of the present. In S. Gilligan (Ed.), *Therapeutic conversations.* New York, NY: W. W. Norton.

White, M. (1995a). Therapeutic documents revisited. In M. White, *Re-authoring lives: Interviews and essays* (pp. 199–213). Adelaide, Australia: Dulwich Centre Publications.

White, M. (1995b). Psychotic experience and discourse (interviewer K. Stewart). In M. White, *Re-authoring lives: Interviews & essays* (pp. 112–154). Adelaide, Australia: Dulwich Centre Publications.

References *(continued)*

White, M. (1995c). Naming abuse and breaking from its effects (interviewer C. McLean). In M. White, *Re-authoring lives: Interviews and essays* (pp. 82–111). Adelaide, Australia: Dulwich Centre Publications.

White, M. (1995d). The narrative perspective in therapy (interviewers D. Bubenzer, J. West & S. Boughmer). In M. White, *Re-authoring lives: Interviews and essays* (pp. 11–40). Adelaide, Australia: Dulwich Centre Publications.

White, M. (1995e). Introduction. In M. White, *Re-authoring lives: Interviews and essays,* (pp. 5–10). Adelaide, Australia: Dulwich Centre Publications.

White, M. (1997). *Narratives of therapists' lives.* Adelaide, Australia: Dulwich Centre Publications.

White, M. (1998). Notes on power and the culture of therapy. In C. White & D. Denborough (Eds.), *Introducing narrative therapy: A collection of practice-based writings* (pp. 228–229). Adelaide, Australia: Dulwich Centre Publications.

White, M. (1999). Reflecting-team work as definitional ceremony revisited. *Gecko: A Journal of Deconstruction and Narrative Ideas in Therapeutic Practice,* (2), 55–82. Reprinted in M. White (2000), *Reflections on narrative practice: Essays and interviews* (pp. 59–85). Adelaide, Australia: Dulwich Centre Publications.

White, M. (2000a). Re-engaging with history: The absent but implicit. In M. White, *Reflections on narrative practice: Essays and interviews* (pp. 35–58). Adelaide, Australia: Dulwich Centre Publications.

White, M. (2000b). Direction and discovery: A conversation about power and politics in narrative therapy (Interviewers Michael F. Hoyt & Jeff Zimmerman). In M. White, *Reflections on narrative practice: Essays and interviews* (pp. 97–116). Adelaide, Australia: Dulwich Centre Publications.

White, M. (2000c). On ethics and the spiritualities of the surface (Interviewers Michael F. Hoyt & Gene Combs) In M. White, *Reflections on narrative practice: Essays and interviews* (pp. 129–161). Adelaide, Australia: Dulwich Centre Publications.

White, M. (2001, March 1) *Narrative Therapy: Delight and Unexpected in Therapeutic conversations* [Video recording]. Michael White Video Archive (Tape 38). Adelaide, Australia: Dulwich Centre.

White, M. (2002a). Addressing personal failure. *International Journal of Narrative Therapy and Community Work,* 3:33–76. Republished in White, M.(2004). *Narrative Practice & Exotic Lives: Resurrecting diversity in everyday life* (chapter 5), pp. 149–232. Adelaide, Australia: Dulwich Centre Publications.

White, M. (2002b, August 6). *Untitled* [Video recording]. Michael White Video Archive (Tape 192). Adelaide, Australia: Dulwich Centre.

White, M. (2003). Narrative practice and community assignments. *International Journal of Narrative Therapy and Community Work,* 2, 17–55.

White, M. (2004a). *Narrative practice and exotic lives: Resurrecting diversity in everyday life.* Adelaide, Australia: Dulwich Centre Publications.

White, M. (2004b). Working with people who are suffering the consequences of multiple trauma: A narrative perspective. *International Journal of Narrative Therapy and Community Work,* (1), 45–76. Reprinted in D. Denborough, (Ed.), (2006).*Trauma: Narrative responses to traumatic experience* (pp. 25–85). Adelaide, Australia: Dulwich Centre Publications.

White, M. (2006a). Fostering collaboration – between families and children, and between child protection services and families. An interview, in M. White, & A. Morgan, *Narrative Therapy with Children and their Families* (pp. 121–136). Adelaide, Australia: Dulwich Centre Publications

White, M. (2006b). Responding to children who have experienced significant trauma: A narrative perspective. In M. White, & A. Morgan, *Narrative therapy with children and their families* (pp. 85–97). Adelaide, Australia: Dulwich Centre Publications.

White, M. (2006c). Children, trauma and subordinate storyline development. In D. Denborough, (Ed.), *Trauma: Narrative responses to traumatic experience* (pp. 143–165). Adelaide, Australia: Dulwich Centre Publications.

White, M. (2007). *Maps of narrative practice*. New York, NY: W. W. Norton.

White, M. (2011a). The Responsibilities: Working with men who have perpetrated violence. In White, M. (2011) [Ed. David Denborough] *Narrative practice: Continuing the conversations*. pp. 98–117. New York, NY: W. W. Norton.

White, M. (2011b). Power, psychotherapy, and new possibilities for dissent. In White, M. (2011) [Ed. David Denborough] *Narrative practice: Continuing the conversations*. pp. 45–70. New York, NY: W. W. Norton.

White, M. (2011c). Bringing the world into therapy and subverting the operations of modern power. In White, M. (2011) [Ed. David Denborough] *Narrative practice: Continuing the conversations*. pp. 3–26. New York, NY: W. W. Norton.

White, M. (2018, June 25). *Michael White, narrative therapist: Funny moments* [video file]. Retrieved from https://vimeo.com/260519508

White, M. (n.d.-a). Untitled. [Video recording]. Michael White Video Archive (Tape 258). Adelaide, Australia: Dulwich Centre.

White, M. (n.d.-b). *Untitled*. [Video recording]. Michael White Video Archive (Tape 244). Adelaide, Australia: Dulwich Centre.

White, M. & Epston, D. (1986). Consulting your consultant's consultant. *Proceedings of the sixth Australian Family Therapy Conference*, Melbourne, Australia 1985.

White, M., & Epston, D. (1990). *Narrative means to therapeutic ends*. New York, NY: W. W. Norton.

Williams. B. D & Baumgartner, B. (2014). Standing on the shoulders of giants: Narrative practices in support of frontline community work with homelessness, mental health, and substance use. *International Journal of Child, Youth and Family Studies*, 5(2): 240–257.

Wingard, B. (1996a). Grief: Remember, reflect, reveal. *Dulwich Centre Newsletter*, (3), 30–35. Reprinted in B. Wingard & J. Lester (Eds.) (2001), *Telling our stories in ways that make us stronger* (pp. 45–55). Adelaide, Australia: Dulwich Centre Publications.

Wingard, B. (1996b). Introducing 'sugar'. *Dulwich Centre Newsletter*, (3), 26–29. Reprinted in B. Wingard, & J. Lester (Eds.) (2001), *Telling our stories in ways that make us stronger* (pp. 19–25). Adelaide, Australia: Dulwich Centre Publications.

Wingard, B. (2010). A conversation with Lateral Violence. *International Journal of Narrative Therapy and Community Work*, 1, 13–17.

References (continued)

Wingard, B. (2002). Stories of pride: Linking the experience of Aboriginal Australia, African-American, Latino and Native American communities. *International Journal of Narrative Therapy and Community Work*, 2, 56–59. Reprinted in Wingard, B., Johnson, C. & Drahm-Butler, T. (2015) *Aboriginal narrative practice: Honouring storylines of pride, strength and creativity* (Chapter 13, pp. 147–152). Adelaide, Australia: Dulwich Centre Publications.

Wingard, B., Johnson, C. & Drahm-Butler, T. (2015) *Aboriginal narrative practice: Honouring storylines of pride, strength and creativity*. Adelaide, Australia: Dulwich Centre Publications.

Index

a

b

c

d